BARKING UP A NEW TREE

Rethinking Dog Training

Bethany Bell

Canine Ethical Associates

Copyright © 2024 Bethany Bell

All rights reserved

No portion of this book may be reproduced in any form without permission from the publisher, except as permitted by U.K. copyright law.

Some characters that are portrayed in this book are fictitious. Any similarity to real persons, living or dead, is coincidental and not intended by the author. All events are true, real events that did happen, but client's names have been changed to protect their privacy.

Cover design by: Bethany Bell
Printed in the United Kingdom.

Dear Fred and Helen Holmes,

I could not have done any of this without your continuous support, love, and guidance. All my achievements are because of you.

To my husband Henry,

You have been my rock, supporting me through all my moments of self-doubt. Thank you for everything! Especially for your help with all my technical tantrums over publishing this book!

CONTENTS

Title Page
Copyright
Dedication
Chapter One – A Life Changing Moment   3
Chapter Two - The Journey Begins   9
Chapter Three – A Difficult Puppy.   22
Chapter Four – New Perspectives   28
Chapter Five – A Dog's Learning Potential.   33
Chapter Six – The Scientific Lens   43
Chapter Seven - What Is Reactivity?   47
Chapter Eight – Individual learning   61
Chapter Nine - Conditioning and Desensitisation   64
Chapter Ten - Language   83
Chapter Eleven - Ethics   93
Chapter Twelve - Choices   108
Chapter Thirteen - Personality and Breed Traits   117
Chapter Fourteen - Understanding Canine Emotions   127
Chapter Fifteen – My Career Change   138
Chapter Sixteen - Heartbreaking decisions   150
Chapter Seventeen - New Chapters   159
Chapter Eighteen – The Future of The CDD Method   166

Acknowledgement	171
About The Author	173

Barking Up a New Tree – Rethinking Dog Training.

Preface

As you turn the pages of this book, you embark on a journey that is as much about discovery as it is about companionship. This book isn't just a collection of thoughts and experiences; it's a reflection of a profound journey with dogs, those remarkable beings who enter our lives in the guise of pets but soon become so much more.

My journey into the world of dogs began not as an expert, but as a learner, a seeker of understanding. Each dog I've had the privilege of knowing has been a teacher in their own right, guiding me through the complexities of canine behaviour and the simplicity of unconditional love. This book is born out of those lessons, out of the countless moments of joy, frustration, learning, and, above all, companionship.

"Barking Up A New Tree" is more than just a title; it's a metaphor for the journey I've embarked upon – a journey of challenging the conventional, exploring new methods, and continuously learning. The Canine Dialogue Dynamics (CDD) method, which forms the heart of this book, is not just a set of techniques; it's a philosophy, a way of life that honours the natural essence of our dogs.

This book is for every dog parent, trainer, professional and enthusiast who has ever looked into the eyes of a dog and seen a soul staring back. It's for those who have felt the deep-seated desire to connect, understand, and communicate more effectively with their dog. Through these pages, I share not only the knowledge and insights I've gained but also the stories and experiences that have shaped my understanding. I wish to make it clear that this book is not about dictating what is right or wrong in the world of Force Free dog training, nor is it intended to cast judgment on current force-free practices. Rather, it offers a space for critical thinking, presenting thought-provoking insights and a fresh perspective on our interactions with dogs. It's an invitation to open-mindedness and empathy, encouraging readers to see beyond conventional methods and explore new, perhaps unconventional, paths.

As you read, I invite you to open your heart and mind to the possibilities that lie within the bonds we share with our dogs. This is a journey of mutual growth, understanding, and love. It's a journey I am honoured to share with you.

Welcome to "Barking Up A New Tree" – a story of discovering, understanding, and loving the dogs in our lives.

CHAPTER ONE – A LIFE CHANGING MOMENT

In the spring of 2020, at the peak of my career as an accredited dog trainer and behaviourist, life threw us a curveball. My husband, who had joined me in the business, and I were nestled in the chaos of the pandemic when our landlord dropped the bombshell: our rental home needed major repairs, and we had to move. We had only lived there a year, but sadly this beautiful home had not been well maintained over the previous years and had reached a point of disrepair.

Moving wasn't new to us – thanks to my husband's previous job, we'd hopped from place to place quite a bit. But this time, the stakes were higher. We had our three dogs to think about, not to mention the pandemic raging outside. Plus, I was gutted about leaving behind the training field we had lovingly built. My husband had fenced it in with sturdy stock fencing, and we'd just installed a secure gate. We'd weathered river floods that swept away my training gear, tackled break-ins, and dealt with endless power cuts. It was a place of both challenges and triumphs.

The mix of emotions was overwhelming: relief at leaving a problematic place, frustration over losing what we had worked so hard to create, fear of moving during a health crisis, and anxiety about finding a dog-friendly rental in the UK's tough market. Financial strains from the property's issues and the pandemic's blow to our business only added to the uncertainty.

Miraculously, we found a charming bungalow to rent. Moving

from Worcestershire to Oxfordshire was bittersweet – we were leaving cherished memories behind but also stepping into a new chapter. That move was a whirlwind of exhaustion, stress, and sleepless nights. The final night before moving, I packed through the darkness while my husband and dogs caught some sleep before the big drive.

Arriving at our new home, emotions I'd bottled up just poured out. Outside, trying to compose myself, I realised how deeply the entire ordeal had affected us. The dogs, too, were visibly shaken by the change. Our new place, opposite a horse training paddock, presented new challenges. With a less secure patio and our spaniels struggling with the new environment, we reluctantly decided to have my parents look after them while we settled in. Our retriever, Joyce, stayed with us due to her separation anxiety.

In this new, quieter setting, Joyce transformed. She was calmer, more attentive, and astonishingly, less reactive. The constant stressors of our previous home – the public footpath, the incessant barking at passersby – were gone. Here, she seemed content, even unbothered by the sounds of horses and people nearby. It was a revelation. Could this peaceful environment be the key to easing her reactivity? Or she could have been shut down, but she didn't express the typical signs, she was in fact the happiest she had ever been!

Joyce, our most challenging rescue, with her myriad of issues, was showing us perhaps what she needed all along was not just training, but a space where she felt safe and unexposed. This discovery was a turning point, not just for Joyce, but in how I approached my work with dogs.

Five days later, the longing for our boys became too much. We planned to reintroduce them to our new home gradually

– Steve first, then Dave the next day. They had been happy with my parents, but it was time to reunite. However, upon Steve's return, an unforeseen calamity struck, shaking the very foundations of our lives.

We introduced Joyce to Steve outdoors, thinking a familiar setting would ease the transition. Joyce was a dog who startled easily, so we wanted to avoid her from startling if Steve were to suddenly announce himself in the new home.

They greeted each other, tails wagging, and we all moved towards the house. They both seemed content. In an instant, the calm shattered. Joyce, in a sudden surge of aggression, pinned Steve to the ground right at the doorstep. The sight of blood against our freshly painted door is an image I'll never forget. Instinctively, I intervened in a way no dog expert would recommend – I gently opened Joyce's jaws to free Steve. My husband, equally shaken, took Joyce for a walk to diffuse the tension while I cared for Steve before Henry rushed him to the vet.

The aftermath left me in a state of shock and guilt. Joyce's uncharacteristic outburst of violence left me questioning everything I knew about her – and myself as a dog owner. Clearly, I had missed something, I had made mistakes that led to this traumatic event. Clearly Joyce was capable of things I didn't comprehend, I always knew any dog can bite, but I had assumed only when treated a certain way or warnings ignored. Could I ever trust Joyce around dogs ever again? I suppressed the temptation to blame her for her actions, with heightened emotions it's easy to feel resentful towards a dog when they hurt you or someone you love. Despite my conflicted emotions, I comforted her, promising silently to find a way through this. I kissed her soft forehead, stroked the ridge of her nose slope, and whispered to her "We will make this better, I promise".

The vet reassured us that Steve's ear could be stitched, with no lasting physical damage. Yet, the emotional toll was evident. The anxiety of bringing Steve back home was overwhelming. Would Joyce react again?

We decided to keep Dave with my parents a little longer, giving us time to address this new, unsettling dynamic. When Steve returned, Joyce's growl confirmed my worst fears – her aggression wasn't a one-off incident. My heart sank lower than I ever imagined possible, with no certainty of what our dog's futures looked like, I phoned a close friend and cried my eyes out.

That night, my husband and I slept in separate rooms, each with one dog, our minds racing with troubling questions. Had our life with them changed forever? Could Joyce and Steve ever coexist peacefully again? The thoughts of rehoming, safety, and fairness to both dogs weighed heavily on us. The uncertainty was agonising.

This incident marked the beginning of a new, challenging chapter in our lives. It was a stark reminder of the complexities and unpredictability of dog behaviour. A reminder that even with experience and knowledge, there are moments that can leave us feeling utterly helpless – but also determined to seek solutions, understanding, and a path forward for the well-being of our beloved dogs.

The next day, we embarked on a quiet, enriching walk with both Steve and Joyce. Managing their interactions carefully, we watched as Joyce remained quite relaxed around Steve, who, understandably cautious, seemed to tread lightly around her. His apprehension tugged at my heartstrings. Gradually, Joyce's aggression subsided, and Steve's wariness lessened. We longed for Dave's presence, and finally, it felt right to bring him back home.

With the lessons learnt from Joyce's previous outburst, we reintroduced Dave in a more thoughtful, prepared manner. Joyce's reception of Dave was lukewarm at best, leaving Dave bewildered by her hostility. Though less aggressive than with Steve, it was clear things had changed. The dynamics among them slowly eased over the following weeks, yet a sense of normalcy never fully returned. We were left emotionally drained, constantly on edge during their interactions.

Confounded by Joyce's behaviour, I reached out to my network of experienced dog behaviourists – colleagues and mentors alike. Despite our collective knowledge, the root of Joyce's guarding issues remained elusive. Veterinary checks, dietary adjustments, and revisiting her history offered no clarity. It dawned on me that despite my extensive training and experience, I was at a loss. Joyce was amenable to training, enjoyed her treats, and engaged eagerly in tasks and games, yet none of these addressed the underlying issues. It was as if we were skimming the surface, making no real progress in understanding her deeper needs.

This crisis of confidence shook me to the core. I questioned my capabilities, pondering a career change. Yet, deep inside, a spark of curiosity and determination refused to die out. I began to question the very foundations of my understanding of dog behaviour. What if there was more to learn, more perspectives to consider?

This introspection led me to a community of professionals who shared my doubts and were exploring alternative, less conventional approaches. I delved into overlooked research, entertained challenging and thought-provoking ideas, and began to see cracks in the conventional dog training paradigms. It was a journey into uncharted territories, one that rekindled my passion and redirected my focus towards a more holistic, nuanced understanding of canine behaviour.

It was during this period of deep reflection and exploration that the seeds of the Canine Dialogue Dynamics method were sown. A method that promised to bridge the gaps I had encountered in my practice and offer a new way to connect with and understand our dogs.

To understand this journey, we need to first understand how it all began at the beginning.

CHAPTER TWO- THE JOURNEY BEGINS

My intrigue in dog behaviour and training ignited when I was 18 and studying Animal Welfare in Basingstoke. A lifelong passion for animal welfare, instilled in me since childhood by my parents, was the fuel. My father, an avid rescuer of snakes, lizards, and even tarantulas, shaped my early experiences with animals. I spent my younger years aiding him in conservation efforts, restoring habitats for native reptiles.

A poignant memory from 2005 remains etched in my mind: a devastating fire at Thursley Common in Surrey. Witnessing the once vibrant heathland reduced to ashes was heart-wrenching. Amidst the despair, a moment of connection with a thirsty lizard that drank from my hand confirmed my path – I was destined to dedicate my life to helping animals.

Raffety, a golden retriever, and Smash, an English Bulldog, were my childhood companions, teaching me the joys of growing up with dogs.

Raffy and Smash, my childhood dogs.

At 15, after a challenging time with bullying in school, I found refuge in an agricultural college near Guildford, studying animal care. It was a turning point – a place where I finally belonged. My teenage years weren't without their ups and downs, but they led me to my future husband. We met at college, and quickly, our lives intertwined.

In 2009, I resumed my studies in Basingstoke, which culminated in a transformative work experience at a dog training school in Chertsey. What began as a short stint evolved into an 18-month journey as a dog trainer's assistant. Here, I was introduced to the world of positive reinforcement and force-free training, setting the foundation for my future career. In a significant and heartwarming shift in my personal life, I found myself moving in with my in-laws, embracing their three delightful welsh terriers. Betty, Ted, and Trevor.

Trevor, One of the three Welsh Terriers.

By 2012, after marrying and moving to Essex, and then returning to Guildford in 2013, I joined a local force-free training facility. Balancing this with my studies, I completed my Level 3 diploma and eventually pursued a degree in Animal Behaviour and Welfare. Completing my degree was a profound achievement for me as I had not found it easy, but my mum had supported and encouraged me throughout all my academic meltdowns!

Each step of this journey enriched my understanding and approach to dog training, guiding me towards a more compassionate, empathetic method that would eventually become the cornerstone of my professional life.

In 2014, the loss of my beloved Raffy to cancer left a void in my heart, a void that deepened when Smash, too, crossed the rainbow bridge a few months later. The absence of their presence was palpable every day. With my husband's career in horticulture flourishing, we decided in late 2015 to embrace a new chapter and find our first dog together. Both of us, having grown up with dogs, felt ready to fill the void left by Raffy and Smash with a new adventure with dogs.

The search for our new family member was an adventure in itself. We debated over getting a puppy or a rescue, pondered various breeds, and finally settled on the idea of a Newfoundland puppy. But fate had other plans. An online advert caught my attention – a Black and Tan spaniel in need of a home. There was an instant connection; I read about his personality and his current behavioural struggles, and I just knew he was meant to be with us. My husband agreed wholeheartedly upon seeing his picture – that happy, lively face was irresistible.

We named him Steve. Bringing him home was an emotional journey. As I stroked his silky fur, he looked at me with those expressive brown eyes, a mix of nervousness and trust. He nestled into my lap, and I felt him relax as we bonded during the drive home.

Steve's previous owners had struggled with his behaviour. They had adopted him and his sister together, but the pair didn't get along. It was clear they loved him, but managing two dogs, particularly when Steve showed signs of reactivity towards other dogs, was overwhelming for them. Steve's bark was robust for his size, and he had developed a habit of chasing shadows and light reflections – not out of stress, but an obsessive behaviour, nonetheless.

Despite my background in animal care and ongoing education in dog training, dealing with Steve's behavioural issues was a new challenge. We made the typical mistakes that many dog owners do in such situations. It was a learning curve, understanding Steve's unique personality and finding ways to address his needs. He wasn't just a dog with issues to be fixed; he was a complex being with emotions, fears, and a distinct personality.

On his first day with us, we allowed Steve the space to settle in at his own pace. His need to be close was apparent, and we welcomed it, perhaps without fully understanding what it meant. In our eagerness, we might have overwhelmed him – introducing him to our family, taking him on long walks, and starting training right away. It's a sobering thought, reflecting on what those initial days must have felt like for him, ripped away from all he knew into a whirlwind of new faces, places, and routines. My interpretation of his affection as immediate trust was perhaps naive; it was more likely a sign of his insecurity and his search for safety in an overwhelming world.

As the week progressed, Steve seemed to be adjusting, but it soon became clear that he struggled with being left alone. Moments of solitude for him were laden with stress and panic, evidenced by his distressing behaviour whenever we returned. Realising this, we stopped leaving him alone entirely. Additionally, house training was an issue – his anxiety often led to accidents in the house, even on our bed. Seeing him cower and wet himself when meeting new people, particularly those who loomed over him, was heart-wrenching. At first, I thought these reactions pointed to a traumatic past, but as I delved deeper into understanding canine developmental stages, I realised it might be linked to his experiences during critical periods of growth.

In an attempt to build his confidence and social skills, we took him to a dog-filled park. However, the experience was far from beneficial – Steve became so agitated, barking uncontrollably. This pattern repeated in public spaces; his reaction to other dogs was extreme, drawing stares and comments from onlookers, making me feel embarrassed and helpless. Eventually, I avoided public outings, choosing secluded areas for his off-lead time. Interestingly, he seemed more at ease with other dogs when not restrained by a lead.

Regrettably, at 14 months old, we made the decision to castrate Steve, clinging to the hope that it might resolve his issues. It was a decision made out of desperation, and one I later learnt in my career wasn't the solution I had hoped for. This experience was a stark reminder that behavioural issues in dogs are rarely fixed with quick solutions; they require understanding, patience, and often, a different approach than what conventional wisdom suggests.

In 2016, our move to Newbury, Berkshire, opened a new chapter in our lives, one where my career in understanding dog behaviour and reactivity took a giant leap. It was during this time, while exploring various dog groups on Facebook, that I chanced upon an advert that would change our lives. A charming black and white spaniel, with unique splotches marking his face, caught my eye. At just 11 months old, he had been through several homes, unable to find a place that could match his boundless energy. The moment I saw him, laying casually across a coffee table with a look of sheer character, I felt a connection. This was Dave, who was soon to become an integral part of our family.

Bringing Dave home, we were apprehensive about how Steve would react, given his history of reactivity towards other dogs. To our surprise and relief, their first meeting was a success – they played together as if they had known each other for years. Dave's arrival brought a sense of completeness to our home, and a sense of comfort to Steve, who seemed more at ease with Dave by his side. Over the next few weeks, Steve felt comfortable being left alone with Dave, he just needed company after all.

As I delved deeper into my studies on dog behaviour, particularly focusing on reactivity and behavioural issues, I found myself learning from a wide array of well-known behaviourists. Through books and courses, I absorbed every piece of knowledge available, eager to apply it to our life with Steve and Dave. Their relationship, like any, had its ups and downs. They had their disagreements, usually over the usual canine disagreements - toys, attention, or the best spot on the sofa. But as they grew to understand each other, a strong bond formed.

Dave, neutered before he joined our family, exhibited a mix of robustness and sensitivity. His reactions to certain stimuli, like the subtle creak of a door or the whisper of the wind, were intriguing, whilst not being bothered by louder, more obvious noises. His way of expressing affection was unique – from day one, he would give genuine hugs, wrapping his front legs around my shoulders in a warm embrace. Initially, these behaviours seemed to stem from insecurity, but as he grew more confident, they became endearing traits of his loving personality.

With Steve, I employed desensitisation techniques to help manage his reactivity. We started at a comfortable distance for him, using high-value rewards and acknowledging every positive response to distant dogs. The goal was to keep him below his threshold, gradually exposing him to his triggers in a controlled manner. This approach, based on keeping him focused on familiar tasks while slowly reducing the distance to his triggers, was a critical part of our journey. It required patience, understanding, and a keen sense of Steve's comfort levels.

Looking back, I realise this phase was essential in shaping my approach to dog behaviour. While desensitisation had its place, I began to see its limitations. It was a method that worked on the surface but didn't always address the deeper emotional layers of a dog's reactivity. This realisation sparked a desire to explore beyond conventional methods, to seek a more profound understanding of the emotional and psychological aspects of dog behaviour.

Throughout this journey, we tried various rewards and environments, teaching Steve different responses to his triggers. Despite our efforts, progress was elusive. Every small step forward was met with significant setbacks. I had read that such setbacks were a normal part of the process, but our stagnation seemed anything but normal. After two years of consistent effort, we were no further along than when we started. In my frustration, I blamed myself, thinking perhaps I wasn't quick enough, prepared enough, or knowledgeable enough. Then, my thoughts turned to Steve, wondering if he was inherently flawed, beyond help. It was a painful conclusion, but I chose to accept and love him as he was, believing that while he might be an exception, the methods I was using could still help others.

In late 2017, my career took a new turn when I joined a charity training assistance dogs for veterans. As an approved trainer, I found great satisfaction in this work, remaining with them until I eventually stepped away from training. My parents also welcomed their new rescue dog, Hank, a wonderful and funny Bulldog.

Dave saying hello to Hank, after a walk together.

2018 marked the beginning of my own dog training and

behavioural business. Starting with 1-1 sessions, behavioural therapy, and classes, the first six months were modest, but soon, the business boomed. I was running classes across two locations, covering everything from puppy training to fun agility. Reactivity was my speciality, and each behavioural client began with a comprehensive consultation and a detailed report covering aspects like diet, rest, enrichment, and more.

The results from using the most popular training methods were varied. Some dogs responded well and quickly, able to focus on their owners or tasks amidst distractions. This was the epitome of success in the eyes of conventional training. However, not all stories were of triumph. For some, progress was painstakingly slow, and for others, it seemed an unreachable goal. It was tempting to attribute these shortcomings to the clients – perhaps they weren't practising enough or following the guidance properly. Yet deep down, I knew this wasn't the whole truth for many cases. Despite growing doubts, I couldn't bring myself to question the methodology I had invested so much in.

Ginny quickly became besties with Steve and Dave!

As I navigated through the complexities of each case, a nagging thought persisted – were we really addressing the root of these behavioural issues? Or were we just applying band-aid solutions to deeper, underlying problems? It was a question that began to gnaw at me, urging me to look beyond the surface, to reconsider what I thought I knew about dog behaviour and training.

This period of introspection and questioning was the catalyst for a profound shift in my perspective. It was the beginning of a journey that would lead me to challenge the conventional wisdom of dog training and seek a deeper, more holistic understanding of canine behaviour – a journey that would eventually culminate in the creation of the Canine Dialogue Dynamics method.

In my practice, I catered to a variety of training requests, primarily focused on general obedience. Utilising treats, conditioning, and positive reinforcement, I guided clients through heel work, recall games, loose lead walking, and other fundamentals. As a force-free trainer, I held myself to high ethical standards. Interestingly, my own dogs, Steve and Dave, didn't fit the mould of typical obedience. Their free-spirited nature was something I cherished, though I didn't fully grasp why until much later. In truth, I found training my own dogs somewhat mundane. Perhaps it was the repetitiveness or my own inconsistency, but my enthusiasm waned, and I preferred to let them enjoy their off-lead freedom.

CHAPTER THREE – A DIFFICULT PUPPY.

In December 2018, a distressing call from a client set another turn of events in motion. She spoke of a young golden retriever puppy, only 14 weeks old, facing the threat of euthanasia for being labelled aggressive after a biting incident. My heart went out to this puppy. After discussions with my husband and realising no one else could take her in, we decided to step in. The environment we collected her from was far from ideal, reinforcing our decision.

Joyce at 15 weeks old, shortly after arriving. (This is not a high tree stump!)

The journey home with her, who we named Joyce, was

heartrending. She howled and barked relentlessly, inconsolable despite our attempts to comfort her. Her arrival at home was met with mixed reactions from Steve and Dave, and the atmosphere was tense. I questioned our decision, overwhelmed by the challenge of managing her intense separation anxiety. Despite every positive training technique I knew, including sleeping in an open crate with her, nothing eased her panic.

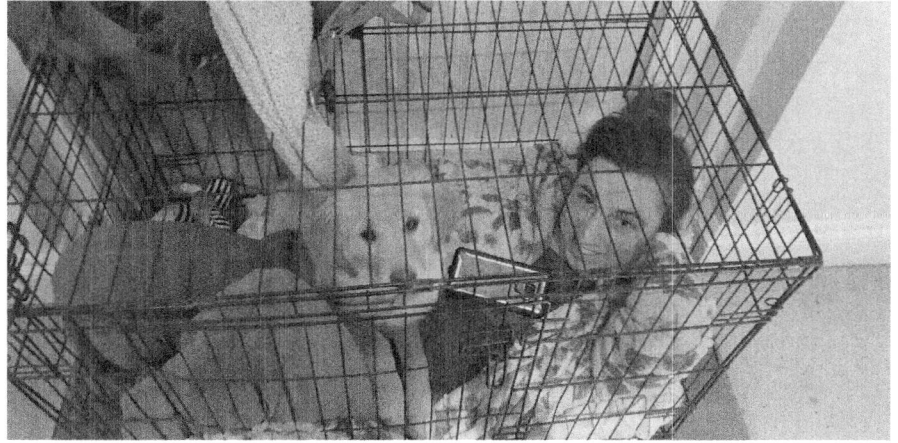

Spending some time in the crate and practicing the door being closed.

Reflecting on those early days, I see how my approach was somewhat naive. I believed that with her young age and my skills, I could resolve her issues through training and behaviourism. Joyce was a complex character – demanding, not overtly joyful, yet not aggressive either. She seemed misunderstood, her natural puppy behaviours mistaken for aggression. I took time off work, hoping to integrate her into our household and ease her anxiety. This period was one of the most challenging I had ever faced. We altered our lives significantly to accommodate her needs, a commitment driven by our determination to provide her with the care and understanding she desperately required.

Joyce's arrival marked a significant turning point in my understanding of dog behaviour. It was a journey that further highlighted the limitations of conventional training methods, especially when dealing with deeper emotional and psychological issues in dogs. Her presence in our lives reinforced my belief that understanding a dog's unique personality and emotional state is crucial. Joyce challenged every single thing I thought I knew about dogs, she taught me so much through her reluctance to use a crate, reluctance to change her personality, her strong sense of entitlement and her willingness to persist in getting what she wanted whenever she wanted it. Although she presented different challenges, and made me feel like a failed dog professional each and every day, I adored her.

Every time I left the room, Joyce's panic was palpable, manifesting in relentless barking. Consequently, toilet breaks, showers, even bedtime routines were reshaped to include our golden pup. My husband and I adjusted to sleeping separately, ensuring Joyce and Steve were comfortable and safe until they were ready to share a sleeping space.

As the New Year approached, I had hoped Joyce would be more accustomed to being left alone, even for brief periods, but that milestone seemed a distant dream. We found ourselves reorganising our daily routines to accommodate her needs – she either accompanied me everywhere or stayed with my husband between his work commitments. It was a difficult adjustment, yet I kept telling myself it was just a temporary phase.

Initially, I walked Joyce separately from Steve and Dave, allowing her individual socialisation experiences unimpacted by Steve's reactivity. She joined the boys for off-lead adventures, but these solo walks were crucial for her social development. She was a natural at making friends, both canine and human, during our visits to local coffee shops and parks. However, as she edged into adolescence around five months old, a shift occurred. She began alert barking at anyone entering the café or approaching us – a development that filled me with disappointment.

Training sessions initially curbed this behaviour, rewarding her for settling down. But this success was short-lived. She soon started reacting to other dogs entering the café, her alert barks escalating. When I used treats to calm her, she became fixated on them, losing focus on relaxing in the environment.

Realising the café visits were becoming too stressful for her, I limited them, choosing settings she could handle. Still, she exhibited defensive behaviour when approached by other dogs while stationary. It was a perplexing regression, mirroring Steve's challenges. As Joyce grew, so did the complexity of her interactions – friendly one moment, overly exuberant the next. It seemed typical teenage behaviour, yet I couldn't help feeling concerned.

By May 2019, Joyce was nine months old, and her separation anxiety showed no signs of abating. Balancing her needs with our growing work commitments and my husband's job was increasingly challenging. We made the tough decision to relocate, with my husband joining the business full-time to help manage Joyce's care. The hunt for a rental accommodating three dogs was daunting, leading us to consider moving further away. We eventually found a suitable home in Evesham, Worcestershire. This move meant a one-and-a-half-hour journey from our previous residence, but it was a necessary step. We maintained our client base in Newbury, managing a three-hour round trip alongside local work, all to keep our business thriving in the face of these new challenges.

Joyce's separation anxiety was intensifying, evolving into a profound distress whenever I was away. Her attachment to me was so strong that even my husband struggled to soothe her in my absence. Despite their enjoyable walks and exploration of new areas, she remained restless and anxious without me. We realised that to care for Joyce adequately, either my husband or I needed to be available at all times, a situation that put considerable strain on both our personal and professional lives.

Our new home in Evesham, situated along a public footpath, introduced fresh challenges. Joyce's alert barking at passersby, especially those with dogs, escalated. Steve and Dave, previously indifferent to such stimuli, began to mirror her behaviour, adding to the cacophony and tension. Joyce was a bundle of contradictions - her bright intelligence, endearing sweetness, and playful nose-boops contrasted sharply with her bouts of anxiety and unpredictability.

Her excellent lead-walking skills provided some solace; she moved with a grace and obedience that was a joy to witness. However, the large glass windows in our new home, offering unobstructed views of the footpath, only exacerbated her stress. We covered as many windows as we could, but her unsettled behaviour persisted. At 11 months old, Joyce experienced her first season, which brought new dynamics into our household, particularly with Steve, who until then had merely tolerated her presence.

During her first season at 11 months old, we kept Joyce away from public areas. Interestingly, her behaviour around other dogs mellowed in the following months, possibly influenced by hormonal changes. A memorable encounter with a tiny Chihuahua puppy, where Joyce displayed remarkable gentleness and restraint, warmed my heart, and filled me with pride. Yet, as time passed, her interactions with other dogs became increasingly unpredictable. This inconsistency eroded the trust I had in her, leading us to limit her exposure to other dogs, much like we had done with Steve.

We applied desensitisation methods, similar to those used with Steve, to Joyce. Initially, she seemed more responsive, eagerly focusing on treats rather than other dogs. But it soon became apparent that this was a mere diversion, not a genuine shift in her feelings towards other canines. Multiple consultations with trusted colleagues and behaviourists confirmed that we were following the recommended approach perfectly, yet the lingering sense of failure was hard to shake. The question haunted me – why couldn't I help my own dogs?

This period of doubt and introspection was pivotal. It forced me to confront the limitations of conventional training methods and question whether they truly addressed the underlying emotional needs of dogs like Joyce and Steve. It was a time of deep reflection and learning, pushing me further towards the development of an approach that went beyond mere behaviour modification. This then takes us back to our pivotal moment of change when we moved from Evesham to Oxfordshire.

CHAPTER FOUR – NEW PERSPECTIVES

As I settled into our new life in Oxfordshire, my quest for deeper understanding led me to explore beyond the conventional boundaries of dog behaviourism. Engaging with the work of professionals who were going against the grain and immersing myself in Jaak Panksepp's research on emotional systems, opened my eyes to a plethora of perspectives I had never considered. Their diverse viewpoints and innovative approaches were instrumental in reshaping my own beliefs and practices.

It was an enlightening yet challenging journey, confronting the myths that had been ingrained in my professional thinking as facts. I had to navigate through my biases, reevaluate long-held beliefs, and let go of my defensiveness towards the conventional methods I had been advocating. This process wasn't just about acquiring new knowledge; it was about fundamentally altering my perception of dog behaviour.

The more I delved into this new field of understanding, the more I realised how many accepted 'facts' in dog training were unproven or misinterpreted. This realisation was both unsettling and liberating, prompting me to question everything I thought I knew. It became clear that the path to true understanding lay in thinking critically, not just accepting widely held beliefs.

One of my biggest hurdles was redefining my relationship with the concept of training. I had always viewed dog training and behaviourism as two distinct yet interconnected fields, each with its variations. However, what I was beginning to understand was that training is just a component of a much broader spectrum of canine teaching and learning.

The conventional definition of training is about imparting specific skills or behaviours, often through repetition and reinforcement. It's a process widely used in preparing dogs for various roles and activities. In contrast, teaching encompasses a broader scope. It involves imparting knowledge, not just skills, helping the learner to understand and interpret information, experiences, and even emotions.

While training and teaching can overlap, they are not synonymous. Training focuses on specific outcomes, often through structured methods and repetition. Teaching, on the other hand, is more about facilitating understanding, guiding the learner through experiences, and encouraging independent thinking and decision-making.

This distinction became a turning point for me. Understanding that training is just one aspect of teaching – an important tool, but not the only one – was crucial. Recognising that not every situation requires training, and that not every dog responds well to training methods, was a significant shift in my perspective.

In the world of dog training, we often lean heavily on repetition to cultivate specific skills. These skills, developed through persistent practice, differ significantly from the broader concept of training as understood in human contexts, such as sports. In the canine realm, we're essentially teaching dogs to perform certain behaviours or movements with precision. This method of training is highly instructional, where dogs learn to obey a sequence of commands through consistent repetition and reinforcement.

The nature of reinforcement in dog training varies; it can be positive or negative, gentle, or strict. My practice, firmly rooted in force-free training, reflected what I believed to be the kindest and most ethical approach. However, my initial understanding was somewhat limited. I hadn't fully appreciated that force in training could extend beyond the physical to include more subtle psychological elements, such as coaxing, luring, or even manipulating.

The dictionary definitions of 'force' include 'coercion or compulsion, especially with the use or threat of violence' and 'making someone do something against their will'. In dog training, these definitions can blur into areas where our intentions, though well-meaning, might inadvertently coerce a dog into actions that go against their instincts or comfort.

For example, consider a situation where an owner encourages a dog to approach something they find intimidating. The dog's instincts urge caution or retreat, but the owner, using high-value rewards or persuasive coaxing, convinces the dog to override these natural inclinations. This scenario, while not overtly forceful, can create a significant internal conflict for the dog. By complying with the owner's wishes against their instincts, the dog learns a form of dependence that might undermine their ability to think and act independently.

This understanding forced me to reevaluate my perspective on training. I began to realise that there's a fine line between guiding a dog and inadvertently exerting a form of psychological force. It became clear that teaching a dog involves more than just imparting skills; it's about understanding and respecting the dog's mental and emotional state, encouraging decision-making that aligns with their natural instincts and wellbeing.

This shift in understanding prepared the way for the development of the CDD method. This approach transcends conventional training, focusing instead on communication and mutual understanding. It respects the dog as a sentient being with their own thoughts, feelings, and instincts. This method fosters a relationship based on mutual respect and understanding, rather than on unilateral instruction and compliance.

This situation, where a dog is encouraged to go against their natural instincts, can arise even with the best of intentions. It's a common practice, often thought to foster confidence and resilience. I too held this belief until I viewed it through a different lens. Training, especially when applied repetitively across all aspects, can become somewhat clinical. It lacks the depth of communication and a broader picture of information that creates understanding, elements that are intrinsic to teaching.

Teaching, in its essence, is educational and instructional, yet it encompasses far more. It's a versatile blend of guidance, information, communication, experience, and understanding. Neither teaching nor training is inherently superior; they are simply different. Used in tandem, they complement each other, weaving together to create a more holistic approach. However, when training is relied upon as singular methods, they can lead to complications.

A dog that depends solely on cues, reinforcement, and instructions may find it difficult to engage their own thought processes, to make independent decisions. Such reliance can inhibit the dog's ability to activate their 'thinking brain', impeding their emotional development and capacity for change. When we utilise rewards to distract a dog from their triggers, the dog's focus shifts to the task of earning reinforcement rather than processing the situation and their emotions. They're not learning to manage their emotional responses or to be truly present in the moment. Instead, they are conditioned to fall into automatic responses, a strategy that only offers temporary respite, as it doesn't address the underlying emotional state.

Over time, this method's effectiveness wanes. The dog, unable to continually suppress their emotions, edges closer to a breaking point. As the emotional mind struggles to maintain control, the instinctual mind takes over, propelling the dog into a state of perceived threat and self-protection. This outcome, unfortunately, is all too common in many dogs subjected to these training processes. It fails to facilitate a genuine change in the dog's mindset and emotional well-being.

This understanding was pivotal in my journey towards developing the CDD method. It became increasingly clear that a dog's emotional and psychological needs cannot be met through training alone. This insight guided me to create a method that emphasises understanding, communication, and respect for the dog's natural instincts and emotional state. The goal was to foster a learning environment where the dog feels understood and respected, where their natural behaviours and emotions are acknowledged and addressed in a manner that promotes true understanding and change.

CHAPTER FIVE – A DOG'S LEARNING POTENTIAL.

Delving into the depths of canine cognition has led me to a profound realisation: the belief that dogs are cognitively equivalent to 2- to 3-year-old human children is a perspective that might be too limiting. This idea, while prevalent, is based on studies that have focused narrowly on specific cognitive abilities, like understanding human gestures or basic arithmetic. However, this doesn't necessarily reflect the complete range of a dog's intellectual capacity.

Take, for example, Chaser, the border collie renowned for her extensive vocabulary. Her ability to understand about 1000 words was akin to that of a 3-year-old child. Yet, this level of linguistic skill is a product of intensive training and doesn't represent the baseline of an average dog's cognitive capabilities. It does, however, open the door to considering the potential for more profound linguistic comprehension in dogs than previously thought.

Evan MacLean's research at the Arizona Canine Cognition Centre has been instrumental in illustrating that dogs excel in cooperative communication tasks, akin to the abilities of 2- to 3-year-old children. But again, these studies may not fully capture the entire scope of canine cognition, often not venturing into comparisons with older children.

The intriguing question then arises: what if we were to compare dogs' cognitive abilities with those of 4- to 6-year-old children? Would we find that in certain areas, particularly in receptive language, dogs might show capabilities that align more closely with this older age group? This area of research is not thoroughly explored, leaving open the possibility for dogs to demonstrate more advanced cognitive abilities in certain contexts.

Moreover, the methodologies and focus of these studies often do not encompass the full spectrum of cognitive abilities for either dogs or children and tend to overlook the distinct evolutionary and environmental factors shaping canine cognition. This narrow focus can lead to an incomplete understanding of dogs' true intellectual capabilities.

Recognising these limitations in current research, it becomes apparent that the theory of dogs being cognitively capped at a toddler's level may not paint the whole picture. We should be open to the possibility that dogs might understand more than we currently attribute to them, needing a more comprehensive and open-minded approach to fully appreciate their intelligence and potential.

In considering the cognitive abilities of a 4-6-year-old child, we find areas where dogs might match their abilities in _receptive_ language. This challenges the notion that dogs can only understand as much language as a toddler, suggesting that there's more to canine intelligence than current literature fully supports. While there are clear differences in cognitive milestones due to species-specific traits, a dogs' ability to understand language and concepts, particularly when taught, implies a greater cognitive capacity than that of an infant.

Exploring the cognitive landscape of dogs in relation to the abilities of a 4-6-year-old child provides us with a fascinating insight into their world of receptive language. This comparison, while not implying dogs have the full _cognitive_ ability of a young child, certainly challenges the outdated notion that dogs are cognitively equivalent to infants. The complexity of their understanding, especially when nurtured through methods like Canine Dialogue Dynamics or similar methods, reveals a depth of comprehension that aligns in certain respects with that of older children. In this comparison I incorporate the use of the word "command" something I am not keen on implementing but it is relevant to this comparison.

Let's delve into this comparison more intricately:

Receptive Language:

- 3-3.5-Year-Old Child: Understands spatial concepts like "in front of" and "behind," differentiates textures and shapes, and responds to commands involving two actions or objects.
- Dogs: Capable of understanding entrances, exits, and the spatial orientation of objects. They can identify basic shapes and even discern colours when taught. Similarly, they can respond to commands involving multiple actions or objects, showcasing a level of understanding comparable to young children.

Expressive Language:

- Children: At this age, children start asking 'how' questions and follow commands with prepositional phrases.
- Dogs: While they can't ask questions, they certainly respond to them, especially when taught specific meanings, indicating a sophisticated level of comprehension.

4-5-Year-Old Child:

- Receptive Language: A child's ability to understand complex sentences and grammar starts to develop.
- Dogs: They can understand nuanced differences in language and more complex sentences, although they do not grasp grammar.

Comparative Abilities:

- Physical Awareness: Both dogs and children at this age understand left and right, and most sentences taught to them.
- Conceptual Understanding: Dogs can be taught the names of their body parts, similar to children who know theirs. However, children's understanding of language structure is more advanced.

5-6-Year-Old Child:

- Receptive Language: Children at this age have a more developed understanding of language. They are capable of grasping more complex sentences and concepts, including a rudimentary understanding of grammar. Their ability to follow multi-step instructions and understand the nuances of language is more advanced.
- Dogs: While dogs cannot comprehend grammar and complex sentence structures like children, they show remarkable abilities in understanding nuanced differences in human language. For example, dogs can respond to more complex phrases and understand a variety of commands that go beyond basic instructions. Their ability to interpret human emotions and respond to them also shows a level of emotional intelligence that parallels older children in certain aspects.

Comparing Complex Understanding:

• Children: Are beginning to understand abstract concepts and can follow more complex narratives.
• Dogs: While not capable of abstract thought or following narratives, dogs can understand a range of commands and cues that involve multiple steps or actions. Their ability to interpret human body language and tone of voice suggests a sophisticated level of social intelligence.

In summary, this comparison illuminates the remarkable capabilities of dogs in certain aspects of cognition, particularly in receptive language and social intelligence. While they cannot match the full cognitive abilities of a 5-6-year-old child, especially in terms of language structure and abstract thinking, their understanding in other areas is profound and often underappreciated. This comparative analysis reveals that dogs, when appropriately taught, can grasp concepts and language in a way that aligns with certain abilities of older children. It underscores the importance of looking beyond the limitations of current research, which often confines dogs' cognitive capabilities to those of younger children.

Science, in its pursuit of understanding canine cognition, often lags behind what many dog owners and trainers observe in practice. As scientific focus shifts to the intricacies of the canine brain, we anticipate further revelations and progress in this field. This ongoing exploration promises to deepen our appreciation of the intelligence and capabilities of our canine companions.

This newfound understanding brings about a significant shift in perspective. Dogs, as mammals with complex mammalian brains, possess thoughts, feelings, emotions, and an innate ability to understand much more than we've traditionally given them credit for. My previous inability to see this might have stemmed from a lack of necessity or awareness. However, the realisation that dogs could potentially have cognitive capacities not fully acknowledged or utilised opens up new horizons in our interactions with them.

The prevailing notion that dogs are limited in their cognitive abilities, akin to those of a young child, has perhaps inadvertently restricted their development. Just as a child's learning and understanding are stunted if they are not progressively challenged beyond their toddler years, dogs too might be experiencing a similar plateau in their cognitive development. This is largely because our methods of communication and teaching with them have been overly simplistic.

In my experience, the common practice in dog training has been to use singular, often one or two-syllable words. This approach, though well-intentioned to avoid confusion, may have inadvertently limited their potential to understand more complex language and concepts. Like many, I would engage in casual, comforting chatter with my dogs, often using a 'baby-talk' style, which was more about providing comfort than truly educating or challenging them cognitively.

However, this realisation that dogs are capable of understanding more sophisticated language and concepts, much like the developmental stages they go through, signifies a need to rethink our approach to canine education. It's not just about training them to respond to basic commands but about engaging with them in a way that stimulates their cognitive abilities, respects their intelligence, and acknowledges their emotional depth.

This shift in understanding calls for a more nuanced and respectful approach to canine teaching, one that goes beyond conventional training methods to truly unlock the potential of their remarkable minds.

The journey of teaching language to dogs was a learning curve for me, involving a process of simplification and natural progression without the use of reward-based reinforcement. This approach wasn't initially instinctive; I found myself overthinking and overcomplicating the task, making it more challenging for both myself and my dogs. The key was to start simple, mirroring the way parents would introduce concepts to children, despite my lack of experience in this area.

The process began at home, where I felt more comfortable. I started incorporating language into our daily routines, using straightforward sentences. For instance, as my dogs waited by the door, I'd say, "Are you ready to go into the garden?" and then let them out. During mealtimes, I'd pick up their bowls and ask, "Are you hungry?" as I prepared their food. The emphasis was placed on key words to help them focus and understand. Remarkably, it took only a few repetitions for them to grasp the meaning of these phrases.

I soon started using anticipatory language, speaking to them before they engaged in an activity. For example, when they seemed tired, I'd suggest, "Would you like to lie here?" or "Do you want to settle down?" aligning my words with their mental state and needs. This approach rapidly became effective, and they soon began to understand their routine through language cues alone.

Most dogs understand the word "walk," associating it with the activity itself. I extended this concept by talking through the entire routine of going for a walk, saying things like "Are you ready for your walk? Shall we go out?" and then responding to their reactions accordingly. I'd narrate each step, like getting dressed for the walk, ensuring to listen and watch for their replies.

Understanding a dog's response is crucial and involves interpreting their body language - tail movements, facial expressions, ear positions, movement direction, and vocalisations. Each dog, being an individual, communicates differently, and body language interpretation isn't static but fluid and context-dependent.

My conversations with my dogs would change based on their responses. If they didn't want to go for a walk, I respected their choice, staying home or leaving them as the situation demanded. This respect for their choices is integral to the CDD method, allowing them to be their true selves and express their unique personalities and breed traits.

This approach of integrating language into daily interactions with dogs isn't just about issuing commands or training; it's about fostering a deeper understanding and connection. It's a journey of mutual learning, where we learn as much from our dogs as they do from us, developing a language of understanding that surpasses conventional training methods.

Adapting to the fluidity of natural communication marked a significant shift in my approach towards my dogs. Shifting away from the rigid consistency typical in training, I began to embrace the diversity and richness of language. It's akin to nurturing a child's vocabulary, where there's no strict adherence to a limited set of phrases. This fluidity in communication allows for a more natural and organic growth in understanding and connection.

I remember moments of doubt, when I would find myself repetitively using the same phrase in specific contexts. This realisation hit me that such rigidity stems from training protocols, where precision and consistency are paramount. However, natural conversation varies with context, employing different phrases to convey similar meanings without being confined to a set script. In teaching language to children, we instinctively use a broad spectrum of vocabulary, allowing for a more holistic development. I aimed to mirror this approach with my dogs.

Even with my commitment to this new method of communication, each instance of my dogs grasping and responding to my words filled me with astonishment. During our walks, I engaged in ongoing dialogues, describing our actions and guiding them towards better choices. An example of this was teaching them to wait at gates between fields. Initially, I would narrate our actions, like passing through a gate, and after a few repetitions, they began to understand the routine.

One memorable day, after their usual energetic play in a safe field, I told them, "When you're finished, wait for me at the gate." To my amazement, they individually made their way to the gate once they had finished sniffing and waited. Their waiting wasn't the static, trained behaviour often seen in dog training. They moved around, sniffing and exploring, yet mindful of my approach. This wasn't about holding a position but understanding the concept of waiting in a natural, contextually appropriate manner.

Their understanding continued to grow, evident in various

situations. For instance, if they wandered too far ahead, a simple "Wait for me to catch up" would have them slow down. Or a gentle reminder, "Stay close to me here," adjusted to the situation and never delivered in the exact same manner.

Experiencing these moments of growing understanding and communication with my dogs was profoundly rewarding. It fostered a deeper bond and connection, far exceeding what I had previously thought possible. This process wasn't just about teaching them commands; it was about developing a shared language, enriching our relationship and their individual personalities.

Joyce and I having a conversation!

CHAPTER SIX – THE SCIENTIFIC LENS

My journey into the world of natural learning for dogs left me both convinced and curious. It was hard to grasp why such a valuable and life-altering approach wasn't more widely known. Keen to delve deeper, I sought to understand the scientific backing for this method, but I quickly realised the limitations of being too reliant on scientific studies. Science, often slow to catch up, can miss out on groundbreaking practices that are observed in the real world.

Take Pavlov's work on classical conditioning, published back in 1897. His findings were revolutionary, yet it took decades for these concepts to be widely accepted and applied in the dog training community. This lag in the adoption of new scientific insights is not unusual. Science, by its very nature, is cautious and methodical, sometimes taking years to validate what practitioners have known and applied for ages. Science is an ever-changing landscape of discovery. One breakthrough that seems definitive today may be reconsidered or even disproved in the future, as new findings emerge. Often, these shifts in understanding are influenced by biases, subtly swaying results to align with a particular narrative. This tendency can mould our perceptions, occasionally overshadowing objective truths in favour of more favoured or convenient interpretations. It's this continuous process of reassessment and evolution that lies at the heart of scientific inquiry, reminding us that our comprehension of the world is always in a state of progression and refinement.

The focus of scientific research on dog cognition has predominantly been within the frameworks of training and behaviourism. However, this focus is just one aspect of understanding our dogs. It's crucial to remember that science is just one part of the puzzle. It should inform and guide us, but not be the sole basis of our understanding. Research on the canine brain, for instance, has been largely framed within these traditional contexts, possibly overlooking other important aspects of canine cognition.

Independent studies have begun exploring how dogs process human language and understand our intentions. For instance, a study from Eötvös Loránd University in Hungary, which used EEG and MRI scans to study canine brain activities, sheds light on this topic. However, even in scientific research, one must be cautious. It's essential to consider who funds these studies and their potential motives, as research can sometimes be skewed by biases or specific agendas.

This revelation was a turning point for me. To embrace a new understanding of canine intelligence, I had to challenge my long-held beliefs and biases. The brain often gravitates towards familiar concepts, reinforcing existing beliefs and making it difficult to accept new ideas. True learning requires stepping out of this comfort zone, examining our biases, and being open to new perspectives and ideas.

So, while scientific studies are undoubtedly valuable, they're not the only source of truth. They need to be balanced with practical, real-world observations and experiences. This balanced approach is crucial for gaining a comprehensive understanding of dogs and their remarkable abilities.

The process of learning and adapting to new methods, like the one I was embarking on with natural learning for dogs, was indeed challenging. There were moments when I would overthink simple concepts or face mental blocks that made it difficult to absorb new information. In these instances, I found it best to take a break, allowing my mind to rest and process what I had learnt so far. This approach was akin to respecting a dog's readiness in facing new experiences, emphasising the importance of natural progression rather than forced learning.

This journey wasn't just about acquiring new knowledge; it was about fundamentally changing my perspective. It took time, patience, and a willingness to let go of long-held beliefs. For me, the entire transformation spanned over two years, partly because life's various challenges often created additional hurdles. However, I noticed that while some of my clients grasped the concepts quickly and applied them successfully with their dogs, others took longer to adjust. This variance only highlighted the importance of moving at your own natural pace, without the pressure of set timelines or unrealistic expectations.

Much of the foundation of the CDD method draws on a variety of already established methods, both from human and canine psychology. Although comprehensive studies specifically focusing on dogs in this context were limited, there was a wealth of research on the human mind that could be referenced. Human psychology, in many ways, has been informed by studies on other animals, including rodents, birds, and some primates. This cross-species learning isn't unusual; in fact, it's been a common practice in psychological research.

Understanding that the principles of psychology often

transcend species lines can be surprising to some. However, it's important to remember that despite the clear differences between humans and dogs, the basic functioning of the mind has similarities across mammalian species. This knowledge allows us to infer certain capabilities and limitations in dogs, using human psychological research as a reference point. Such an approach not only broadens our perspective but also enriches our understanding of canine behaviour and cognition.

CHAPTER SEVEN - WHAT IS REACTIVITY?

Steve is barking his happy shout here!

Reactivity, often described in the dog world, has become a somewhat misapplied label. Initially, it was meant to indicate a specific response to stimuli. Now, it broadly labels any canine behaviour that doesn't align with societal norms or seems disproportionate to the context. This generalisation is misleading. There aren't inherently 'reactive' dogs. Rather, dogs react according to their perceptions and emotions, a natural response to their environments.

By definition, being 'reactive' encompasses two aspects: responding to stimuli and reacting to a situation rather than proactively changing it. Every living being exhibits this reactivity as part of being conscious and aware. However, in the context of dogs, the term has been skewed, suggesting an inherent problem with the dog. This mislabelling impacts people's perceptions, leading to misconceptions about the dog and their owner. It often results in judgement, avoidance, or criticism, reinforcing fear and insecurity in owners. They feel isolated and unsure, often fearing judgement and questioning their ability to support their dog.

This misinterpretation of 'reactive' has significant consequences. It overlooks the individuality of each dog and the real reasons behind their reactions. However, instead of viewing a dog's reaction as a deep-rooted issue to be corrected, applying understanding, and empathetically addressing the specific causes can lead to more effective and compassionate outcomes. This approach recognises each dog's unique needs and emotions, fostering a deeper understanding and connection between dogs and their humans.

When dogs struggle to cope in certain situations, their reactions might resemble our own responses to fear or stress, such as barking, trying to escape, or showing agitation. These behaviours are often labelled as 'reactive', a term that has gained a somewhat negative connotation, suggesting something is wrong with the dog. However, this label doesn't always take into account the individual reasons behind each dog's behaviour. Looking at a dog's reactions as a means of communication is a more accurate way of understanding reactivity. What are they saying? Are they trying to tell us something or someone else? Why are they saying it in this manner? How must they be feeling right now? Are questions that will lead you to a more accurate conclusion to what is happening. I am not suggesting that the word reactive or reactivity is bad, but the understanding of what these words entail is coming from the wrong perspective.

In psychology, various methods like desensitisation, counterconditioning, and avoidance are used to address fears. These methods have been adapted for dogs, but they don't always address the root cause of a dog's fear or anxiety. Desensitisation involves controlled exposure to the fear source, while counterconditioning aims to change the dog's emotional response. Avoidance simply means avoiding the fear-inducing situation. Though these can be effective, they often treat only the symptoms, not the underlying issue.

A more comprehensive approach involves understanding each dog as an individual, recognising their specific triggers and their unique emotional responses. This means observing the dog's behaviour and identifying the situations that cause distress. It's also important to consider the impact on the dog's human companions, who might experience similar emotions in these situations. Of course, these elements are also applied to more modern desensitisation approaches too.

Effective support for dogs dealing with fear or anxiety isn't just about managing their external reactions. It's about helping them, and their owners navigate through underlying emotions, build resilience, and develop healthier responses to stressors. This process involves rehabilitation and strengthening the bond between the dog and their owner, aiming for a happier, more relaxed life for both.

The key is to avoid generalisations and treat each dog as an individual, tailoring the approach to their specific needs and experiences. This holistic method acknowledges that each dog's experiences and reactions are unique and require personalised attention and understanding.

For clarity, I'll continue to use the term 'reactive dog', though it's important to understand what this really signifies. 'Reactive dogs' often are experiencing a state where their mental capacity is overwhelmed. They find themselves unable to adapt or respond appropriately to their environment. This isn't just a challenge; it's a deep struggle for them. Their minds enter a state of manic stress, where the emotional aspect overrides their capacity for rational thought. In this heightened emotional state, the instinctual part of the brain takes charge, shutting down the intellectual mind – the part responsible for reasoned decisions. This instinctual part is all about survival, lacking the ability to process thoughts. It's the fight-or-flight response in action. When a dog reaches this point, their capacity to focus or heed our guidance diminishes. They become survival machines, unable to relax or behave suitably for the situation at hand.

To truly grasp why our dogs, behave the way they do, it's essential to understand both their unique personalities and their inherent breed traits. It's a common misconception that breed-specific traits can be trained away or suppressed. In reality, attempting to suppress these natural behaviours can have adverse effects on a dog's mental state, leading to frustration, confusion, and even depression. Certain breeds are inherently more 'reactive' due to their specific breeding. For example, guard dogs are bred to react to certain stimuli or situations in a way that's quite distinct from breeds not selected for these traits. Terriers, bred for hunting smaller animals, display a natural tendency to be more responsive to small animals and quick movement. Recognising and accepting these breed traits is crucial for truly understanding our dogs.

It's important to note that while we can't change these ingrained traits, we can guide our dogs to better manage their instincts and emotions. We can teach them to exercise self-control and maintain a state where their intellectual mind prevails over their emotional impulses. For some dogs, this might mean learning to quickly soothe their emotional responses, allowing them to move on from initial reactions more swiftly. For crossbreeds, understanding the mix of traits they may have inherited is key to understanding aspects of their responses and behaviours.

Steve and Dave, for instance, have always had a strong instinct to chase birds. Previously unmanageable, this instinct is now within their control. They'll give chase, but only in safe environments, and are much more responsive to my cues, breaking off the chase as needed. Joyce, a suspected mix of Golden Retriever and some shepherd breed, displayed a fascinating blend of traits. Parts of her behaviour were quintessentially Retriever – her playful gait, love of food, and some gun dog characteristics. Yet, she also showed traits typical of shepherd breeds – a protective nature, guarding behaviour, and a switch from alertness to relaxation. This duality in her behaviour highlighted the complexity of understanding a dog that embodies more than one set of breed traits.

Understanding a dog's personality is just as crucial as understanding their breed traits. Even within the same breed, individual dogs can exhibit varying degrees of reactivity. This variability is often seen in working breeds; for instance, some Collies may be less suited to herding than others of their breed. This variation can stem from differences in their lineage, the quality of breeding, and their unique experiences, but it's their individual personality that ultimately defines who they are meant to be.

Each dog possesses a unique personality, distinct from their breed characteristics. When we truly get to know our dogs, we come to appreciate their individuality. This understanding allows us to adapt aspects of our lives to better suit them, akin to how we would for a friend or a child. Dogs, like humans, exhibit a range of personality traits. Some are outgoing, social butterflies with an optimistic outlook on life, revelling in meeting new dogs, greeting strangers, and thriving in bustling environments. Others are more reserved, sensitive, and prefer quieter settings where they can take things at their own pace.

However, personalities are not always straightforward. A dog can be confident yet occasionally shy, or outgoing but still enjoy solitude. This complexity is what renders each personality distinct and individual. We can foster and enhance positive traits in our dogs, but fundamentally changing their core personality is neither feasible nor desirable, much like with ourselves. A naturally shy person, for example, can learn to navigate social situations with more confidence, managing their anxiety without altering their intrinsic introverted nature. They learn to balance their personality, enhancing strengths and managing weaknesses, but the essence of who they are remains constant.

My own personality, for instance, is impulsive and emotionally driven. This trait has its advantages and disadvantages, and while I can't change this fundamental aspect of who I am, I have developed skills to manage my impulsiveness, bringing much-needed balance to my life. We all have our strengths and weaknesses, and our actions can either enhance or diminish these traits.

Similarly, our dogs can flourish when we accept and embrace them for who they are. Allowing them to express their true selves is crucial for any positive change or development. Just like people, dogs deserve the opportunity to be loved and appreciated for their unique characteristics. By understanding and respecting these individual traits, we can create a harmonious and fulfilling relationship with our canine companions, celebrating their uniqueness, and guiding them gently towards a balanced and happy existence.

As a trainer and an owner, I've often found myself hyper-focused on the vocal aspects of reactivity. It's easy to leap to the conclusion that if a dog barks excessively, they must be in distress or frustration. However, this isn't a one-size-fits-all diagnosis. The key lies in understanding the dog's personality, their unique way of expression, and interpreting their body language within the context of the situation.

Take Steve, for instance. His relentless barking for a ball isn't born out of frustration, but rather sheer excitement and joy. Much like a child bubbling with eagerness to show their mum something exciting, Steve's barking is his way of expressing his anticipation and happiness. Understanding this, we found that providing him with something to hold or catch during walks channels his enthusiasm in a positive way, being mindful not to exhaust his joints with excessive ball launching. It's fascinating how getting to know him helped me realise his barking was an expression of happiness, not discontent.

I recall a client who was convinced their dog was highly stressed and reactive due to his incessant barking on walks. This dog's behaviour initially perplexed me. He was noisy, throwing his head back and barking joyously along the path, regardless of the environment. His owners, having tried various training techniques to no avail, were at their wit's end. Yet, he seemed fine with other dogs, people, cars, and animals, with no discernible triggers for his behaviour.

After reviewing video footage of his walks with my colleague, an enlightening revelation hit us. Contrary to my initial assumption, the dog wasn't stressed or reactive. He was simply brimming with happiness and excitement. It turned out his breed was known for being vocal, something I hadn't considered due to my unfamiliarity with this particular breed. My initial perspective, clouded by the common belief that excessive barking equates to reactivity, had blinded me to the obvious. Revisiting the footage with fresh eyes, I saw a dog whose voice and body language exuded openness and relaxation, akin to a chatty, content child. This experience underscored the importance of understanding and embracing a dog for who they are, including their breed characteristics, rather than trying to suppress or change their innate tendencies.

For dogs whose 'reactivity' is not rooted in joy or expressiveness, understanding their mental processes, and addressing their dysfunctional behaviour becomes imperative. This requires a compassionate, kind, and genuine understanding of their emotional state. When we connect with our dogs' emotions, it transforms our approach, imbuing it with empathy and patience.

Owning a dog perceived as 'reactive' can be an emotional rollercoaster. I've felt the embarrassment of aggressive outbursts towards other dogs, the disappointment of public scenes, the isolation from social dog walks, and the envy towards seemingly well-behaved dogs. The guilt that follows, coupled with a sense of failure, can be overwhelming. Initially, I believed I understood canine emotions enough to address reactivity, focusing primarily on fear and anxiety. The common approach of building confidence through positive associations seemed logical - a form of desensitisation involving controlled exposure to triggers, followed by a reward to foster a positive state of mind.

However, this method's reality was far from the theoretical

promise. When it seemed effective, it was often a case of the dog being so conditioned to the distraction that they either ignored the trigger entirely or suppressed their emotions for a reward. This unintentional outcome of desensitisation and counterconditioning revealed a significant flaw in the approach, one that was often overlooked due to our conditioned beliefs in its efficacy.

Instead of viewing reactivity as a problem, it's crucial to empathise with how our dogs experience it. Fear and anxiety are heightened by unpredictability and the unknown. Dogs, not typically taught language, are left to predict what might happen, often feeling insecure due to their lack of understanding. This is where the power of narration comes in, offering reassurance and clarity.

When I started using more natural dialogue with Steve, not just around his triggers but in everyday situations, we saw remarkable progress. On noticing a trigger, his initial reaction was to freeze, unsure of what to do. But through simple, reassuring conversation, acknowledging his concern, and offering an alternative focus, we could navigate the situation with much less stress. For example, upon sighting another dog, I might say, "Oh yes, Steve, there's another dog, but he's far away. Shall we turn back towards the lake instead? It's okay, you don't have to meet him if you're not ready." This approach, grounded in language he understood, provided him with context, reassurance, and a clear understanding of what was happening and what was about to happen.

Each dog and situation require a tailored conversation, depending on the context and the individual dog's personality and needs. But the core principle remains the same: understanding and communicating with our dogs in a language they comprehend can transform our approach to addressing reactivity and other behavioural issues.

Acknowledging our dogs' emotions and feelings is pivotal in helping them feel understood. This recognition shouldn't be an afterthought but a fundamental part of the process. However, it's crucial to note that acknowledgment is most effective when done before our dogs reach a state of meltdown. In such intense moments, they are beyond the point of rational thought. It's akin to how we, as humans, feel when someone validates our feelings; we feel heard, understood, and more equipped to tackle our challenges. This empathy is equally beneficial for our dogs.

The essence of reassurance lies in offering choices and respecting the dog's readiness. It's counterproductive to offer comfort while simultaneously pushing them into situations they're not prepared for. Let's consider a personal fear, like my own fear of wasps. The buzzing sound and their intrusive presence heighten my anxiety. I react by flapping my arms, perhaps screaming or whining, creating quite a scene. The common advice to stay still, meant to discourage the wasp, often leaves me frozen in fear, feeling more vulnerable as the wasp buzzes around, threatening to sting. My heart races, and any sudden movement by the wasp can trigger a panic response, leading me to run without regard for my surroundings. This reaction activates my instinctive mind, making me jumpy and hyper-alert, even towards ordinarily benign things.

This analogy extends to how we sometimes handle our dogs' reactivity. Asking them to remain still while their trigger passes can place them in a similarly vulnerable state, triggering panic and activating their instinctive, fight-or-flight response. In this heightened state, their brain becomes hyper-vigilant, leading to reactions towards things they would normally ignore.

The conventional approach to overcoming fears, like my fear

of wasps, mirrors the desensitisation process often used with dogs. Imagine I'm restrained, much like a dog on a lead, and a wasp is present. I'm offered my favourite treat, let's say pieces of fudge, as a distraction. The goal is to focus on the treat or follow instructions, despite my anxiety. This method might temporarily shift my focus from the wasp, but it doesn't change my feelings about it. It's a temporary diversion, not a solution, and it doesn't prepare me for unexpected encounters or situations where the conditioned response isn't feasible.

This realisation highlights the limitations of traditional desensitisation methods. It shows that simply distracting a dog (or a person) from their fear doesn't fundamentally alter their feelings or prepare them for real-life scenarios. It underscores the need for a more holistic approach, one that truly addresses the emotional states and individual needs of our dogs. This understanding is key to developing methods that respect and cater to their innate feelings, leading to more effective and compassionate outcomes.

Reflecting on the methods I employed to address Steve's reactivity, it's now clear to me how his emotional needs were overlooked. We initially turned to food and toys as distractions from his triggers. Then, we progressed to the engage and disengage game, allowing Steve to observe his trigger before he became uneasy, then calling him to look away and rewarding his disengagement. Despite these efforts, including complete avoidance and rest days to manage his cortisol levels, Steve's threshold for reacting to other dogs remained inconsistent and unpredictable. It was a cycle of two steps forward, one step back.

Steve, much like Joyce, was incredibly trainable. We engaged him in a variety of activities – from agility and tricks to recall and lead games – all of which he excelled at. However, when another dog appeared, all his focus on these activities vanished. No distance seemed far enough to keep him from becoming fixated and frenzied. Despite our dedicated conditioning and desensitisation efforts, complemented by a high-quality diet, enriching activities, ample rest, routine vet checks, and a loving home environment, we hit a wall. It seemed we had ticked every box for a happy, well-cared-for dog, yet it wasn't enough to overcome his reactivity.

After two years of persistent training, I reached a point of exhaustion. Balancing hours of training other people's dogs and applying these methods to Steve, only to see negligible progress, drained my enthusiasm. We had managed to achieve some level of control – sometimes he'd be distracted by food if a dog was distant enough, or he'd break his fixation for a conditioned response after repeated practice. But that was the extent of our success.

Consequently, for a few years, we chose to avoid taking Steve to places where he would likely encounter other dogs while on the lead. Off the lead, he was a different dog, able to play, recall away when uncomfortable, and explore freely. Running is his joy, his release. He is an athlete at heart, and I had to come to terms with the fact that Steve didn't want to be continuously trained. He wanted, needed, to run. This realisation led me to reevaluate our approach and accept that perhaps what Steve needed wasn't more training, but an environment and lifestyle tailored to his innate needs and desires. Sometimes, acknowledging a dog's true nature and providing them with what they instinctively crave can be more beneficial than any structured training routine.

In my journey of understanding canine behaviour, particularly reactivity, I've come to realise the intricate balance between what is often categorised as "fear reactivity" and "frustration reactivity." When analysing Steve's reactions and emotions, and similarly in the cases of many dogs I've worked with, I've noticed that these emotional states aren't always mutually exclusive. Sometimes, it's a blend of both fear and frustration; other times, it's distinctly one or the other. This observation underscores the complexity of canine emotions – they aren't simply black and white but exist in a nuanced spectrum. The concept of frustration reactivity intrigued me. These dogs aren't thought to be necessarily fearful but are overwhelmed with frustration, when denied the opportunity to greet other dogs. Upon greeting, their reactive tendencies often dissipate, suggesting a fulfilment of their desire to interact. However, the disproportionate response to such situations led me to ponder deeper. Is it merely excitement, or could there be an underlying layer of anxiety or uncertainty? The heightened interest in other dogs, particularly evident in adolescent dogs who are still learning to regulate their impulses, partially explains this. But it doesn't always paint the complete picture. Could it be possible that these dogs are, in fact, dealing with internal anxiety about potential threats, which is momentarily relieved upon realising the other dog is not a threat? The distinction between excitement-driven reactivity and problematic behaviour is crucial. An excited dog might vocalise or pull on the lead in anticipation of greeting another dog – this is often normal, especially in younger dogs. However, this isn't necessarily problematic reactivity. Factors like brain development stage, hormonal levels, diet, and exercise play a significant role in managing such excitement. Teaching them to control their heightened emotions and impulses forms a large part of addressing this behaviour. Yet, it's important to note that over-excitement can often be misconstrued as anxiety or fear, as their outward expressions can appear similar. The key lies in interpreting a dog's body language. An open, relaxed posture indicates a genuine greeting, whereas a tense, strained, and overly intense demeanour often signifies defensive behaviour stemming from fear or anxiety. This understanding has led me to recognise that while fear and anxiety are the most prevalent emotions in reactivity, they are not the only reasons for a dog's reactive behaviour. Dogs struggling to cope with heightened emotions require a different approach, one that addresses their unique emotional landscape. This highlights the importance of a tailored, empathetic approach in managing reactivity, ensuring each dog's individual needs are met and understood.

CHAPTER EIGHT – INDIVIDUAL LEARNING

Reflecting on my journey with Steve and his word association, I began to integrate simple sentences into all aspects of our lives. This approach wasn't limited to Steve; I applied it with Dave and Joyce too, each responding in their own unique way.

Dave was remarkably receptive. When faced with choices, he communicated his preferences clearly and decisively. For instance, when asked to wait by the door while I prepared for our walks, he would dutifully do so, exhibiting an innate understanding of my requests. His response to my verbal cues was akin to a beautifully choreographed dance – a seamless blend of listening and responding, with his own individuality. It was as if every dialogue sparked a series of fireworks in his mind, a display of understanding and connection. What struck me most was his ability to discern when to follow instructions for safety and when he could assert his own will. This discernment was crucial, as I yearned not for robotic obedience, but for a relationship where both our voices mattered. Dave's attentiveness and anticipation of my next words were not just acts of compliance; they were signs of a deep, thoughtful bond. He would look back at me on our walks, checking in and attentively awaiting my next words. He has never been trained to check in, this is something he had developed naturally through the use of language and choices.

Steve, on the other hand, required a bit more patience and time to process and respond. His mind was like a racing engine, always in high gear, partly due to his OCD tendencies which often led to compulsive behaviours. We progressed gradually, building upon the language he had already started to grasp. Steve's forte was in responding to directional cues. He might not have been one to lock eyes with me during conversations, but I learnt to appreciate his way of staying engaged.

This realization marked a significant shift in my understanding. I found myself questioning the conventional expectation: why should Steve need to lock eyes with me every time I speak? His manner of engagement, though different, was no less meaningful. I learnt to recognise his presence in his own way – attentively listening while still engrossed in his toy, or while exploring a captivating scent. It dawned on me that his world doesn't need to come to a standstill at my every word. Steve taught me that communication isn't just about demanding undivided attention; it's about mutual respect and understanding, about appreciating his way of connecting while immersed in his own canine joys. His responses were subtle, a gentle reminder that communication doesn't always require grand gestures. Over time, I began to understand the nuances of his movements, each micro-expression revealing a part of his inner world.

Joyce was a blend of contrasts. She picked up on simpler sentences with ease, excelling in tasks like lead walking and recalling in various situations. On the lead, she was a vision of grace, often drawing admiring glances from passersby. Her golden fur shimmered, and her tail swayed with a contented rhythm, embodying the elegance of a show dog. However, this serene picture would abruptly change the moment Joyce encountered a dog she found disagreeable. In an instant, her elegant stride would transform into aggressive pulling and lunging, a stark contrast to her usual poise. Accompanied by a cacophony of barks, snarls, and snorts, her behaviour would shift dramatically, painting a vivid picture of her discomfort and agitation. The startled expressions of onlookers, who just moments ago admired her grace, would morph into looks of dismay and concern. In those moments, my heart would sink, a mix of pride turning into a deep sense of shame and embarrassment. With flushed cheeks and a heavy heart, we'd retreat from the scene, leaving behind a trail of what might have been, overshadowed by the reality of the present. These instances were poignant reminders of the unpredictable nature of our journey, a journey marked by highs and lows, triumphs, and challenges, in our continuous quest to understand and support our beloved Joyce.

These experiences with Steve, Dave, and Joyce have reinforced a crucial lesson: our dogs are individuals, each with their own personalities, preferences, and ways of communicating. Understanding and respecting these differences is key to a deeper, more meaningful relationship with them. It's not just about training them to behave in a certain way; it's about listening to what they're trying to tell us, even when their communication challenges our expectations or desires.

The more I thought about it the issues with conventional training, the more questions it raised. How many other people are facing the same disheartening struggles with applying modern training practices to their dog's behaviour? Why does it seem to help some dogs but not others? Why is counter conditioning and desensitisation so widely used and widely accepted when they clearly have flaws? Were there a whole group of people who felt they were the problem instead of the method itself? It must be so lonely to feel that this method didn't work for you but be led to believe that it worked for so many others. I decided to break down conditioning and desensitisation and rather than take it at face value, I would learn about it in finer detail and then apply it to real life scenarios to expose the flaws it has. It needed critical thinking to be applied.

CHAPTER NINE - CONDITIONING AND DESENSITISATION

Firstly, it's important to recognise that conditioning, far from being something to shy away from, is an integral part of natural learning. This process happens organically as a part of life. The story of conditioning in the domain of dog training is a captivating one, stretching back to the early years of the 20th century. It's a story that orbits primarily around the concept of "Classical Conditioning," a theory brought into the limelight by Ivan Pavlov, a notable Russian physiologist.

Let's examine a brief, yet intriguing overview of this journey:

1. Ivan Pavlov and Classical Conditioning (Early 1900s): The foundations of classical conditioning were laid by Pavlov's insightful observations with dogs. He noted an intriguing phenomenon: dogs would begin to salivate upon seeing the lab assistants who regularly fed them. Curious to explore this further, Pavlov began a series of experiments where he would ring a bell before presenting food. In time, the dogs started to link the sound of the bell with the anticipation of food, salivating at the sound alone, even in the absence of food. This showed how a seemingly unrelated stimulus (the bell) could become a signal eliciting a natural response (salivation), when paired with a stimulus that naturally causes that response (food).

2. John B. Watson and Behaviourism (1910s-1930s): Watson,

building upon Pavlov's groundbreaking work, pioneered the behaviourist school of psychology. He championed the idea that all behaviours could be shaped and moulded through conditioning. His most notorious experiment involved a young child, known as Little Albert, who Watson conditioned to develop a fear of a white rat – an experiment that, while illuminating, raises ethical questions.

3. B.F. Skinner and Operant Conditioning (1930s-1950s): Skinner brought a new dimension to the field with his concept of operant conditioning. This method focused on voluntary behaviours, as opposed to the involuntary responses at the heart of classical conditioning. Through his experiments, notably with the "Skinner Box," Skinner demonstrated how behaviours could be modified more effectively through positive reinforcement (rewards), rather than punishment – a notion that was, at the time, revolutionary.

4. Application in Dog Training (Mid-20th Century Onwards): From the mid-20th century, these principles of conditioning began to be more systematically applied in dog training. Trainers came to realise that encouraging a dog with positive reinforcement – be it treats, praise, or affection – when they performed a desired behaviour led to more fruitful and consistent outcomes.

5. Modern Developments (Late 20th Century to Present): In our current era, the principles of conditioning are widely embraced within the dog training community. The preference leans heavily towards positive reinforcement, coupled with an enriched understanding of canine psychology and behaviour. Training techniques have evolved, becoming more nuanced, focusing on creating environments conducive to positive learning experiences for dogs.

This historical overview highlights a pivotal shift in dog training philosophies – a move away from dominance-based methods to approaches that are more humane, grounded in science, and respectful of the dog's psychological and emotional well-being. Conditioning, in both its classical and operant forms, plays an instrumental role in the methodologies of modern dog training.

Natural conditioning occurs in a dog's life, they are the subtle, yet powerful parts of life that are integrated not through deliberate training, but through the organic associations they form with their environment. This phenomenon mirrors what Pavlov uncovered in his lab, yet it unfolds in the rich, everyday experiences of our dogs, without any orchestrated human intervention. Let's explore some examples:

1. Response to daily routine items: The simple joy of a dog at the sight of their lead. Their tail starts wagging, and they head towards the door, their entire body language exuding anticipation. This response isn't trained; it's a natural association they've formed, linking the lead to the delight of walks. Similarly, the sound of a food container or the rustle of a treat bag can send them into a state of eager excitement. These everyday sounds have become synonymous with mealtime, eliciting an almost Pavlovian reaction.

2. Reaction to household sounds: The everyday sounds of a household can become significant cues for dogs. The familiar hum of a car pulling into the driveway might signal the return of a beloved family member, prompting the dog to eagerly wait by the door or voice their excitement through barking. Similarly, the chime of a doorbell or the knock on the door becomes a herald of visitors, triggering a cascade of reactions born from their associations with these sounds.

3. Seasonal or environmental cues: Dogs, much like us, respond to changes in their environment. The first flurries of snow or the patter of rain can evoke distinct reactions based on their past experiences. For some, snow might mean exhilarating playtime, igniting excitement, while for others, rain might be associated with discomfort, causing apprehension.

4. Emotional responses to human behaviour: Dogs are remarkably attuned to our emotions and body language. A dog might develop nuanced responses to their owner's moods. Observing signs of distress or anger in their human can lead a dog to become subdued or anxious, reflecting their learnt association of these emotions with certain outcomes or atmospheres in the home.

5. Adaptation to schedules: Dogs often seamlessly sync with the rhythm of their household's routine. They might exhibit signs of restlessness as their usual walk time approaches or gently wake their owners at the same time each morning, having internalized these regular patterns as part of their daily life.

These natural conditioned behaviours are a testament to the depth and adaptability of dogs. They reveal an innate capacity to observe, interpret, and respond to the myriad stimuli in their environment, forming associations that subtly guide their actions and reactions.

However, challenges emerge when the focus shifts to intentional conditioning for specific behaviours, especially when a dog's learning revolves predominantly around such responses, rather than being led by their natural behavioural inclinations. It's a delicate balance between guiding their learning and respecting their innate tendencies, a dance of understanding and respect for the individuality of each dog.

Looking into the intricacies of conditioned responses, both in humans and dogs, reveals a fascinating, yet often overlooked, aspect of behaviour. When our brains – whether canine or human – become conditioned to react in a specific way to a particular cue, our natural ability to make choices can be significantly diminished. The conditioned response tends to overshadow our genuine thoughts, emotions, and preferences.

Consider your own life experiences. Have you ever found yourself in the grip of a conditioned response that felt almost involuntary? Perhaps it's the automatic reach for a biscuit when you make a cup of tea, despite not feeling hungry, or the compulsion to check your phone when you hear a notification ping, even if you're in the middle of a conversation. These are classic examples of how conditioning can embed certain habits within us, often ones we'd rather not have.

In these scenarios, our rational mind, which might want to choose a healthier snack or maintain focus on the person we're conversing with, finds itself overridden by the power of conditioning. The habit becomes so ingrained that it feels almost out of our control. It's as if our choice to think and act differently in response to the familiar cue is taken away from us.

The key to breaking free from these ingrained patterns lies in mindfulness and self-awareness. It involves recognising the cue as it arises or anticipating its occurrence. For us humans, it might mean pausing before reaching for that biscuit or consciously deciding not to check our phone immediately. By applying mindfulness to these situations, we can begin to dismantle the automatic nature of the conditioned response. It's a journey of regaining control over our actions and choices, and in the context of dog training, of helping our dogs to do the same. This approach fosters a deeper understanding of our behaviours and opens the door to more conscious and deliberate responses, both for ourselves and our dogs.

In our journey with dogs, we often encounter a complex interplay between naturally occurring conditioned responses and those deliberately trained. Recognising that conditioning can often override the rational part of the brain, it becomes evident that this might similarly impact our dogs, affecting their ability to engage in rational thinking, decision-making, and emotional regulation.

Let's explore this: when we train our dogs to perform a specific behaviour upon a given cue, are they truly able to think beyond that cue? Can they assess whether they genuinely want to engage at that moment, whether they're feeling overly emotional, anxious, or simply not in the right headspace? Or are they, in the throes of conditioning, responding impulsively to the cue, regardless of their emotional state?

I've observed this particularly in dogs grappling with anxiety or fear. The reinforcement of their conditioned response sometimes leads them closer to situations or individuals that clearly unsettle them. It's a delicate balance to strike – understanding when a dog is genuinely at ease and when they're just performing a learnt behaviour, masking their true feelings. Often, their body language might suggest contentment – a wagging tail, what appears to be a smile – but a closer look, especially into their eyes, reveals the true story. It's in their gaze that we often see the tell-tale signs of discomfort, the subtle clues that hint at their underlying unease.

This understanding calls for a more mindful approach to training and interacting with our dogs. It's about recognising and respecting their emotions and mental state, rather than solely focusing on their behavioural responses to cues. By doing so, we open a window into their world, seeing beyond the surface of conditioned responses to the nuanced spectrum of their feelings and needs. It's a journey that not only deepens our connection with our dogs but also enriches our understanding of the complex beings they truly are.

As I analysed deeper into observing the dynamics of dog training, primarily those centred around conditioning, I stumbled upon an intriguing observation. Even amongst the most cheerful and resilient dogs, the interaction and communication between them and their humans often felt somewhat stilted, almost unnatural. Standing on the sidelines, no longer the one offering training advice, this peculiarity struck me with fresh clarity. This style of teaching, heavily reliant on conditioning, seemed clinical and somewhat disconnected from the natural interactions both the person and the dog might otherwise engage in.

Let's pause and consider one aspect in particular – communication in dog training. It's commonplace to use concise, one or two-syllable words as cues, frequently paired with gestures. Pondering over this minimalistic use of language, I couldn't help but find it peculiar, almost surreal in its execution. Here are the key things that stood out to me upon closer examination:

• The cues were predominantly instructional, lacking the natural inflection and richness that usually accompany spoken language.

• The delivery of these cues often had a neutral tone, devoid of the emotional nuances typically inherent in human speech.

• The accompanying gestures were purely functional, like pointing, holding up flat hands, or beckoning – void of the expressive gestures we normally use in communication.

This method of interaction reminded me of the rigid, regimented training of soldiers in the armed forces. Imagine engaging in a conversation in such a manner. It would undoubtedly feel odd and disconnected, making it challenging to grasp the context or the reasons behind the actions requested.

Contrast this with the natural dialogue between a parent and a child. The difference is stark. The parent-child interaction is rich in emotional cues, tone variations, and expressive gestures, creating a deeper, more intuitive understanding.

This observation led me to question the very essence of the behaviours we teach and cue in dogs. Reflecting on my time running classes, I found myself pondering: Why had I taught these behaviours? Why had I not questioned the rationale behind them? Why does a dog need to sit on cue, or lie down when told? Why must they walk unnaturally close to our hip, contrary to their natural walking style? Why are they encouraged to place their paws on inanimate objects, or perform tricks for our entertainment?

These questions opened a doorway to a broader contemplation of dog training – not just as a series of actions and reactions, but as a complex, multifaceted interaction that perhaps needed re-evaluation and a more thoughtful approach, one that respects and embraces the natural behaviours and inclinations of our dogs.

Breaking down these questions further, I reflected on why commands like "sit" and "lie down" are often seen as essential life skills. We typically instruct our dogs to adopt these positions in various settings, such as relaxing at a café or resting on a park bench. But is it necessary for a dog to be sitting or lying down to feel relaxed? Reflecting on this, I realised that when my dogs are at ease, they don't necessarily stick to one particular position. They might stand, lie, sit, walk, or even sniff around, yet still remain perfectly relaxed and content. Similarly, we humans don't confine our relaxation to just one or two postures. We have a whole spectrum of ways to express how comfortable we feel. Imagine if we were conditioned to sit upright or lie down in a specific manner when you're in a 'relaxing' environment. Would that really make us feel at ease, or rather the opposite?

This line of thought reminded me of the challenges I faced with Joyce when she was a puppy. I attempted to guide her into what I thought was a 'relaxed' posture, but it seemed anything but relaxed. While I wasn't overly strict about how she positioned herself, allowing her to shift and take breaks, with ample rewards, the whole process still felt somewhat contrived. I had used a combination of lures and timed reinforcement to achieve the desired sits and downs, without any forceful methods. Yet, I couldn't shake off the feeling that it all seemed a bit forced.

Similarly, I had trained Dave to wait on his mat while I prepared food, to prevent him from jumping at the kitchen counters or begging during meals. He had become so accustomed to this routine that he would automatically lie down on his bed or mat whenever I entered the kitchen, anticipating a reward for his patience. This raises further questions: What if they don't actually feel relaxed or calm? Are we merely conditioning them to mimic these states without genuinely experiencing them?

With Joyce, it became evident that her calm appearance was just a façade. The true indicators were her fixation on the reward, her impatience and frustration when the rewards weren't given continuously, her eager anticipation, and the agitation she displayed at any interruption during training. Some dogs might genuinely relax in these settings, but it's crucial to discern whether they are truly at ease or merely 'opting out'. You can gauge this by observing their overall mood and demeanour. If they're genuinely relaxed, they will respond to your interactions in a calm manner. However, if they seem uninterested or suddenly break from their 'relaxed' state into a hyper-aroused mode, it's a sign they might not be as comfortable as they appear.

Another training activity that seemed odd to me was 'Paws on'. Exploring the concept of confidence building in dogs through interaction with various objects raises intriguing questions about its efficacy. The practice of teaching dogs to place their paws on different objects, such as yoga blocks, wobble boards, skateboards, and mini trampolines, is often believed to enhance their confidence. Initially, I embraced and taught this approach, convinced of its benefits. However, upon deeper reflection, I began to question the underlying logic. How exactly does encouraging a dog to interact with these objects translate to an overall increase in confidence?

In my classes, I observed dogs interacting with a range of objects. While I don't believe there's anything inherently wrong in teaching dogs to engage with these items, especially if they enjoy the activity, I've come to reconsider the notion that it broadly builds their confidence. If a dog is initially hesitant about an object, they might learn to overcome this specific anxiety through positive and careful training. In this context, they do indeed become more confident about interacting with that particular object, whether on cue or sometimes voluntarily. However, this doesn't necessarily translate to a broader increase in confidence in all aspects of their life.

An anxious dog learning to place their paws on various objects might become more adept at this specific task, but it doesn't inherently resolve their general anxiety or lack of confidence. While such activities can undoubtedly be fun and engaging for the dog, implying that they will universally result in a more confident dog might be misleading.

It's crucial to recognise that these activities are context-specific and may not apply to every dog. The idea that such training will universally produce a more confident dog is a misconception. The truth is that confidence building in dogs is a complex process that extends beyond the scope of simple tasks and interactions. It involves understanding each dog's individual needs, fears, and preferences, and working within that framework to build true confidence that permeates all aspects of their lives. Therefore, while 'paws on' training can be an enjoyable and beneficial activity for some dogs, it should not be viewed as a one-size-fits-all solution to building confidence.

When I stepped back from these structured training protocols and reinforcements, I gained a new perspective. Peeling back the layers of trained behaviours revealed underlying unmet needs. Joyce, for example, wasn't relaxed because she felt anxious about people and dogs invading her space. She needed to feel safe and secure, with reassurance that no one would harm her or intrude upon her space.

Dave, on the other hand, was driven by his frustration with food, longing for more enriching and aromatic meals. His food was not satiating enough for him, but the smell of our food was incredibly enticing.

What this exploration uncovered was that training, while useful in shaping certain behaviours, could sometimes mask the true emotional needs and desires driving a dog's actions. Simply training an alternative behaviour doesn't eradicate these innate feelings and impulses; it simply conceals and suppresses them.

To address Joyce's anxiety and unease, I found that providing her with reassurance and acknowledging her concerns was key. By talking her through what was happening or about to happen, she began to feel more comfortable. It became clear that she was communicating her feelings to me, and it was my responsibility to help her navigate these emotions. Adopting this approach, her anxiety and distrust gradually diminished. She started to understand my words and their meanings, and over time, her worries about her surroundings lessened, allowing her to relax more naturally. If she seemed uneasy, we simply left the situation, reinforcing the idea that she didn't have to participate if she didn't feel up to it.

For Dave, who exhibited impulsive behaviour around food, introducing a more varied diet proved effective. Consistently eating the same food can be dull, after all. We began to include more of our food in his diet and eventually started preparing home-cooked meals for him, a change that all our dogs appreciated. This shift led to a noticeable decrease in his food-related intensity and an improvement in his self-restraint. He learnt that waiting patiently for his freshly prepared meals was far more rewarding.

Some might fear that catering to their dog's desires could reinforce negative behaviour. It's a valid concern, but it's based on a misunderstanding. Let's consider this from a more contemporary viewpoint on dog psychology. Depriving our dogs of their wants, under the guise of being the leader or maintaining control, can leave them feeling powerless. A dog without the freedom to make choices in safe situations may feel controlled, leading to erratic behaviour or becoming subdued and suppressed. Conversely, when we respond to their desires appropriately, they feel understood and in control. This doesn't mean we should allow them to do or have whatever they want without limits. Like children, dogs require thoughtful boundaries, structure, routines, and self-regulation to thrive.

The key is balance – providing enough freedom for them to make choices, yet ensuring there is structure and guidance. The more guided freedom we offer our dogs, the less they feel out of control. The less freedom we offer our dogs, the more they feel out of control.

By focusing on meeting our dogs' needs, listening to them, and fostering a team spirit, we saw significant improvements in their behaviour, without the need for conventional training methods. Of course, there were other challenges that required a more structured approach, but that's a story for another chapter!

Desensitisation is another approach that needs exploring more, I had encountered many issues with this approach, and I was keen to understand why it wasn't working for us.

The history of desensitisation in dogs, a technique widely used in behavioural therapy, is closely tied to developments in psychology and animal behaviour science. Here's a brief overview:

1. Early Observations (Pre-20th Century): Observations of animal behaviour suggesting desensitisation likely date back centuries. Farmers, hunters, and animal trainers would have noticed that repeated exposure to certain stimuli could reduce fear or aggressive responses in animals.

2. Classical and Operant Conditioning (Early 20th Century): The work of Ivan Pavlov and B.F. Skinner on classical and operant conditioning provided a foundation for understanding how animals, including dogs, learn and adapt their behaviours in response to stimuli. Although not directly focused on desensitisation, their research helped establish principles that would later inform desensitisation techniques.

3. Systematic Desensitisation (Mid-20th Century): Joseph Wolpe, a South African psychiatrist, developed the concept of systematic desensitisation in the 1950s, initially as a method for treating human phobias. This approach involved gradually exposing the subject to a fear-inducing stimulus in a controlled manner, starting with the least fearful scenario and gradually increasing the intensity.

4. Application in Veterinary Behaviour (Late 20th Century): The principles of systematic desensitisation began to be applied more rigorously in veterinary behaviour and dog training. This shift was part of a broader movement towards more humane, science-based animal training methods. Trainers and behaviourists started using controlled exposure to stimuli to help dogs overcome fears, anxieties, and phobias.

5. Integration with Counter-Conditioning (Late 20th Century to Present): Desensitisation is often used in conjunction with counter-conditioning, a method where a positive stimulus is paired with the fear-inducing stimulus. This combination is thought to be particularly effective in changing a dog's emotional response to a stimulus.

6. Modern Developments and Understanding (21st Century): The understanding of canine psychology and behaviour has continued to evolve. Modern techniques of desensitisation are more sophisticated, often involving a comprehensive assessment of the dog's behaviour, environment, and history. There is also a greater emphasis on the welfare and emotional state of the dog, ensuring that desensitisation processes are conducted in a humane and stress-free manner.

Desensitisation in dogs, as a formal technique, is relatively recent and is part of the ongoing evolution in animal behaviour science. The question arises: does the approach of teaching alternative behaviours truly address the core issues of a dog's behavioural problem? Why do so many dogs, along with their humans, struggle with this concept? This method seemed ineffective with Steve and, while it appeared successful with Joyce, executing perfect behaviour, it didn't address the heart of her issues. It failed to alter her perception or feelings about her triggers. As previously mentioned, desensitisation, often combined with counterconditioning, involves various techniques, such as teaching alternative behaviours to be performed in the presence of a trigger. Fun games like "find it", where high-value treats are scattered away from the trigger, or training games like "middle", "paws on", "look at me" or chase games, are common. The underlying principle is to distract the dog from the trigger, associate something positive with it, and ensure they remain below their threshold, avoiding trigger stacking or flooding. Exposer is part of desensitising dogs, exposing them gently and gradually to their triggers. The objective is to alter the dog's response to triggers, thereby changing their emotional reaction. However, this doesn't always happen.

For dogs where this approach has been effective, there's no issue with continuing it. However, several factors need consideration. Can the dog still function effectively without the specific cues or anticipation of reinforcement? If not, it's likely the dog's core emotional state remains unchanged, and they've just learnt to suppress and hide their true feelings. Some dogs, particularly those eager to please, are adept at exhibiting the right emotions. They will do what their beloved human asks, regardless of their own feelings. This makes them prone to conditioning, entering an automatic mode without genuinely processing or overcoming their issues. When the conditioned cues and/or reinforcements are removed, they're at a loss, unable to cope. Even after attempting to wean them off this reliance, most dogs struggle to succeed. Weaning off a dependency requires acknowledging and resolving the underlying reason for it, a step often missed in desensitisation. Consequently, when the cues and rewards are phased out, and they have nothing else to fall back on, regression often occurs.

This phenomenon is similar to human behaviours, such as snacking on sugary foods, smoking, or habitually reaching for that extra glass of wine. Many people fall back into their old habits when trying to break a dependency because they haven't addressed the root causes of their behaviour. They haven't developed the coping mechanisms and skills needed to manage without their substitute dependency, often reverting to their initial coping mechanisms. However, desensitisation is often approached differently for people compared to dogs. In human therapy, it's usually combined with cognitive behavioural therapy or other methods focusing on understanding the underlying issues and building conscious awareness to develop coping mechanisms. This contrasts with the application of desensitisation in dogs, where it doesn't necessarily foster self-regulation skills; instead, it conditions them to rely on external factors when they're unable to cope.

As I mulled over these challenging realisations, a flurry of questions bombarded my mind. I took my time to process these thoughts, seeking clarity on how to apply them in real-life scenarios. I considered each question, analysing how they related to practical situations. For instance, consider the concept of gradual exposure to triggers. If a dog is conditioned to follow cues, can they genuinely make a considered, independent decision about their proximity to a trigger? Can they autonomously decide to step back, or do we wait until they exhibit unmistakable signs of distress? Wouldn't it be more insightful if we could interpret our dogs' signals earlier? But to truly understand their communication with us and their environment, we need to observe their unconditioned and natural responses. This allows us to comprehend their genuine feelings, needs, and choices, unobstructed by human-imposed conditioning.

The second question I contemplated was the extent of choice involved in determining our dogs' exposure to triggers. While we might believe we're guided by them – noting when they can no longer focus on cues or reinforcements – the reality is we decide where to walk them, often guiding them near or past triggers with cues and encouragement. If a dog is willing and able to focus on the cues, they might comply, but this isn't a genuine choice. What would their behaviour look like without these cues? How would they act if taught to make thoughtful choices? Many assume that a dog would naturally react negatively or place themselves in problematic situations. However, when a dog reacts to triggers or acts thoughtlessly, is this a conscious choice? We know that when a dog is in a state of hyper-arousal or panic, they're not using the thinking part of their brain. Instead, their emotional response activates their instinctual brain, propelling them into fight or flight mode. A true choice stems from the intellectual part of the brain, where decisions are made rationally and thought through carefully. This can't happen concurrently with conditioned, automatic, or unconscious thinking.

This experience reminded me of a complex behavioural case I encountered a few years ago. A distressed family approached me after their dog had unexpectedly attacked another dog during a training session. Fortunately, no physical harm occurred, but the incident left everyone involved understandably shaken. They had been diligently following the training protocols of a local qualified behaviourist and sought a second opinion to understand what had gone awry. After an in-depth behavioural consultation and learning about the dog's history and lifestyle, I concurred with the original behaviourist's methods of counter conditioning and desensitisation. The dog was well-loved and cared for, and seemed to be responding positively to the training, showing no signs of discomfort or aggression even as another dog approached. The dog's needs were seemingly being met, and their dog had already been thoroughly checked by the vets and issued a clear bill of health.

However, in a split second, the situation escalated. The other dog, seemingly uninterested, provoked an intense reaction. My new clients, despite being vigilant and informed, didn't see any warning signs. The attack was brief but startling. While they recounted this event with certainty, the possibility of missed cues or an undetected change in their dog's mood prior to the incident couldn't be ruled out. However, their thorough understanding and detailed explanation led me to believe they had indeed captured the event accurately.

After collaborating with their behaviourist, we were still unable to pinpoint the exact cause of this spontaneous aggression. It wasn't until years later, with a renewed understanding of dog behaviour, training, conditioning, and desensitisation, that a plausible explanation emerged. My hypothesis, although never entirely verifiable for this past event, suggests that the dog had become so conditioned to respond to training cues that he wasn't fully processing his environment. He was partially aware of the approaching dog, but his focus on training overshadowed his awareness. When the trigger suddenly became more apparent, his instinctive fight or flight response was triggered, leading to the unforeseen aggression. This reaction was not a conscious decision, but an automatic response deeply ingrained through his instincts.

This insight, though retrospective, was enlightening. It highlighted the potential dangers of relying solely on desensitisation and underscored the importance of understanding the limitations of conditioning. At the time, I reassured the family it wasn't their fault, but without this newfound perspective, the reasoning behind the dog's behaviour remained elusive, likely leaving them with lingering doubts.

This case reinforced my belief in the necessity of critical thinking, questioning widely accepted dog training methods, and recognising their potential pitfalls. While it would have been easier to conform to the conventional wisdom of the dog training community, the responsibility to those misled by these methods compels me to challenge the status quo and advocate for a more nuanced understanding of canine behaviour. This commitment, though challenging, is essential to providing the most effective and compassionate care for dogs and their owners.

CHAPTER TEN - LANGUAGE

A select group of dog professionals were beginning to acknowledge that dogs might possess a greater understanding than we had previously credited them with. This group questioned the efficacy of relying solely on simple one or two-syllable commands for canine communication. A groundbreaking study, particularly one conducted in Hungary using MRI technology, was pivotal in this realisation. This study revealed that dogs could comprehend language far more complexly than we had imagined. Initially, I must admit, this concept was met with my scepticism, challenging the bedrock of my understanding of canine cognition.

The question arose as to why this particular idea had not immediately resonated with me. Why did it stir such doubt and scepticism within me? Perhaps the real question wasn't whether dogs could understand language, but why I found it hard to believe they could. To address my scepticism, I delved into understanding core beliefs and how rejecting new information can be a natural defence mechanism when confronted with challenging concepts. This process often involves critically examining our existing knowledge and beliefs, questioning their validity and openness to new insights.

As I grappled with this paradigm shift, I realised that the hesitation stemmed from a conflict with the foundational knowledge I had previously acquired. Each of these core beliefs needed to be scrutinized and reassessed. Could they truly stand up to this new evidence, or had they become outdated in light of recent discoveries? This introspective journey was not only about embracing new scientific findings but also about re-evaluating and possibly reshaping my long-held convictions about canine intelligence and communication.

I endeavoured to reconcile these two conflicting beliefs to ascertain which was more logically sound. Firstly, let's consider the notion that dogs cannot comprehend language. To maintain this belief, one would need to assume that dogs possess a limited level of intelligence, capable only of understanding the most rudimentary forms of language. The common viewpoint is that dogs respond to words based on repetition and conditioning, inferring meaning from the sounds and contexts of familiar words. This perspective implies that a dog's capacity for learning and intelligence is somewhat basic and confined.

However, this notion seems overly simplistic when considering the diverse range of abilities dogs exhibit. Intelligence should not be gauged solely on a being's capacity to understand language or perform specific tasks; it encompasses a wide spectrum of skills and capabilities. If we view dogs as creatures that operate only through a series of conditioned cues and instructions, are we not underestimating their intelligence? Surely, the remarkable feats dogs are known for – such as detecting cancer, finding lost individuals, and even sensing impending thunderstorms – contradict this limited view of their cognitive abilities.

Dogs have demonstrated time and again their ability to accomplish tasks that even humans find challenging, often without formal training. Their extraordinary sense of smell, acute hearing, and heightened awareness of their surroundings far exceed our capabilities. While it's true that some of their skills, like scent detection, are innate and surpass human abilities, this doesn't necessarily mean their overall intelligence is as limited as we often perceive. The fact that dogs can interpret body language more accurately than many humans, sense emotions, and adapt their behaviour to different situations indicates a level of understanding and adaptability that goes beyond basic learning.

Having embraced the notion that dogs might have a greater understanding of language than previously believed, I pondered the next question: do dogs actually exhibit this capability? It required some contemplation. Typically, dogs don't spontaneously respond with full understanding to human language unless they've been trained and cued to respond to specific words. However, could there be instances where they demonstrate an understanding of language without explicit training? The more I considered this, the clearer it became that dogs do indeed show us glimpses of comprehension, though we often overlook these moments.

Consider the interactions between dogs and their people. Many dog owners naturally converse with their pets, not necessarily expecting them to understand every word, but because it feels instinctive to communicate with a living being we share our lives with. While the full meaning of such dialogues might not be entirely grasped by the dog, as they were not deliberately taught, there are clear indications that dogs do pick up on the words we use. The simplest examples include dogs showing excitement when asked if they are hungry, or visibly preparing for a walk upon hearing the word "walk". They often display a response when they hear that a favourite person is about to visit. We've all had those moments, often saying in half-jest, "How do they know what I mean?" and then casually brushing it aside. This level of understanding, though partially a result of natural conditioning and association between words and subsequent actions, is fundamentally how language is acquired and comprehended. It begins with basic word association, then progresses to understanding narrative content, eventually applying these learnt concepts in diverse and varied contexts.

Looking back at the study, this groundbreaking research was conducted in Hungary, where scientists used MRI technology to study dog's brain responses to human language. The study involved training a group of dogs to lie still in an MRI scanner, a remarkable feat, considering the natural restlessness of dogs. Once in the scanner, the dogs listened to their trainer's speech. The researchers carefully observed the brain patterns that emerged as the dogs were exposed to various words and intonations.

What the study uncovered was truly fascinating. The dog's brains processed words in a way remarkably similar to how human brains do. They demonstrated the ability to differentiate between known words and nonsensical words, regardless of intonation, suggesting a level of understanding beyond mere tone or emotional cues from their human counterparts. This finding was pivotal in challenging the long-held belief that dogs respond primarily to the tone of our voice rather than the words themselves.

Moreover, the study revealed that dogs processed the emotional content of the words in a different brain region from the one used to process meaning. This distinction is crucial as it mirrors how human brains decipher spoken language, where meaning and emotion are processed separately yet simultaneously.

This research opens up new avenues in our understanding of canine intelligence and their ability to understand human language. It challenges us to rethink the depth and complexity of our communication with our canine companions, suggesting that they are not just responding to our tone or body language but are also grasping the essence of our words to a certain extent.

The implications of this study are profound, inviting us to explore further the cognitive abilities of dogs and how we can enhance our interactions with them through more mindful and meaningful communication. It stands as a testament to the untapped potential in dogs just waiting to be discovered and appreciated.

Although the study in question was conducted with a relatively small sample size, its findings are nonetheless powerful and profoundly thought-provoking. They serve to reinforce what many dog owners have intuitively felt about their dogs – that they do indeed possess a significant understanding of our world, including aspects of human speech. This revelation doesn't just affirm the anecdotal experiences of countless dog lovers; it also facilitates for a deeper appreciation of the cognitive capabilities of our dogs. These insights challenge us to consider the extent to which dogs comprehend not just the tone and emotion in our voices, but also the specific words and meanings we convey. It's a compelling reminder of the complex and rich inner lives that dogs lead, often surpassing our conventional understanding of animal intelligence. While it's clear that dogs don't grasp conversational language to the same extent as adult humans, it's becoming increasingly evident that they can comprehend more natural spoken language, once it has been taught to them, akin to the language understanding capabilities of a young child. Drawing parallels between the cognitive abilities and understanding of receptive language of dogs and children. It seems reasonable to liken a dog's language comprehension to that of a 4-6 year old child. This comparison fits well with the previously discussed similarities in cognitive functioning between dogs and young children, suggesting a level of linguistic understanding in dogs that, while not as advanced as in humans, is still remarkably sophisticated.

Reflecting on the conclusions drawn from logical reasoning and the study's findings, I found it increasingly difficult to maintain my initial scepticism. However, stepping aside from both the logical analysis and the study momentarily, let's ponder the potential impact of adopting this approach in canine communication. What if we aligned our ethical values with the way we interact with dogs? What if, instead of simply training them to react to conditioned verbal and non-verbal cues, we tried to teach them language in a more natural, conversational manner? Would there be any detriment in this approach?

Considering this question, I could only foresee positive outcomes. Our dogs relish being spoken to and engaged in our activities. They thrive on the familiar and comforting sound of our voices. Communicating with them in a way that goes beyond the conventional training methodologies could enhance their understanding and deepen the bond we share with them. It's not about issuing commands; it's about engaging them in a two-way dialogue that acknowledges their intelligence and emotional depth. This approach could potentially enrich their lives, providing mental stimulation and a sense of inclusion that training methods may not fully offer.

Indeed, numerous studies have highlighted the cognitive capabilities of dogs, illustrating their sophisticated understanding and problem-solving skills. While scientific research is invaluable, it's important to remember that studies can sometimes be influenced by the biases of researchers. Therefore, it's essential to balance our reliance on scientific findings with our own logic and reasoning. Anecdotal evidence and personal observations can also play a crucial role in understanding canine behaviour and intelligence. Relying solely on scientific studies can sometimes limit our perspective, as real-world experiences and observations offer valuable insights that may not be captured in controlled research settings. This holistic approach allows us to form a more rounded understanding of dog's capabilities and behaviours.

With this newfound understanding and perspective, I began teaching my dogs starting with word association, building from words and routines they were already familiar with. I used narration, emphasising and timing the words to connect with a particular item, action, or movement. Once they learnt this process, I incorporated the words and concepts into simple sentences. I was amazed at how quickly they picked up these associations, without the need for repetitive training. Once they demonstrated understanding, I no longer needed to teach them that word, as they already knew it. This is when I used the word in different contexts.

Initially, I didn't completely abandon the training methods I had relied on for years. Without a clear picture of an alternative, I gradually reduced the training where I felt comfortable and focused on my new method in areas where I felt confident. This journey was challenging but immensely rewarding. I immediately noticed changes in my dogs. They found learning new words, concepts, and sentences genuinely enriching. Their demeanour changed; they were more thoughtful, engaged, and not just mechanically going through a set of behaviours. The experience was more enjoyable for all of us, free from rigid rules or specific movements.

Over time, we stopped training altogether. We didn't need treats or excessive control. Our dogs learnt faster, demonstrated their abilities more clearly, and showed parts of their personalities that had perhaps been suppressed. This natural dialogue and holistic teaching style allowed them to properly assess what was being conveyed. It was no longer simplistic commands, but language rich with meaning, complemented by natural body language, tone of voice, and context.

However, it wasn't just about talking to them. The words and teachings needed to have true depth and meaning. A one-way dialogue isn't much fun or different from training. So, I learnt to read their responses, understanding that each dog has their own unique 'voice' and body language, more complex than what generic pictures of dog body language depict. For example, flattened ears don't always signify fear; they could mean a variety of things depending on the context. The key is to consider the whole context of their body language and what's happening around them.

I began by asking simple questions like, 'Are you hungry?' or 'Shall we go for our walk now?' Each dog responded in their unique way. Steve was polite, heading to the door for a walk or to the kitchen for food. Dave was more expressive, his bark tone clearly indicating his wants, although sometimes a bit over-enthusiastic, nearly knocking food off my lap. Joyce, our golden diva, was cheeky yet clear in her communication, booping her nose into our hands or swaying her hips towards what she wanted. Her tail movements and facial expressions were particularly expressive.

This approach transformed our relationship. It turned training into a meaningful conversation, respecting each dog's individuality and encouraging a deeper understanding between us. It was a journey from control to mutual respect, from training to true communication.

It was about more than just communication, as I learnt to appreciate when my dogs said no to something. When Dave defiantly refused a task, or Joyce deliberately chose to avoid something she didn't want to do, while Steve would pretend he hadn't heard me. These actions are often labelled as signs of disobedience in traditional, and sometimes even modern, training methods. But my husband and I never sought out only obedient rescue dogs. The times I truly needed my dogs to respond promptly were for genuine safety reasons. In these situations, they could sense the urgency in my voice and would 'obey'. They understood when I was urgent due to potential danger or when a situation could be easily avoided.

But in any other scenario, why should they instantaneously do what I say? What if we reframed 'disobedience' as 'un-submission'? This shift in perspective is profound. I certainly don't want my dogs to be submissive to me, conforming without question or robotically performing tasks. That would suppress their personalities. I don't wish to dampen their spirits. My dogs have the right to say no when it's appropriate. They have the right to express their needs, even if it might seem inconvenient to us. They have a right to use their voice and be heard. This is how a strong sense of self is formed, encompassing self-awareness, self-confidence, and trust.

Consider a typical day with Dave, Joyce, and Steve. If I suggest a game or an activity and they show no interest, I respect their choice. Dave might choose to lounge in the sun instead, Joyce might prefer to play with her favourite toy, and Steve might be more interested in exploring the garden. This approach not only respects their autonomy but also enriches our relationship. They're not just pets following commands; they're individual beings with their own preferences and personalities.

This ethos is at the heart of how we interact with our dogs. It's not about asserting dominance or demanding blind obedience; it's about mutual respect and understanding. Recognising and respecting their right to say no, to express preferences, and to be themselves, we build a deeper, more meaningful connection with our dogs. They learn to trust us, knowing that their voices are heard, and their choices respected. This is the essence of a compassionate and ethical approach to dog care – one that values and celebrates the unique spirit of each dog.

A moment captured - Steve is listening to my words attentively

CHAPTER ELEVEN - ETHICS

Throughout my career, I've always upheld my ethical beliefs to cause no harm in dog training, principles rooted in the force-free training community. This community, comprising ethically motivated professionals, aims to better the dog world, and I am proud to be part of this movement. However, new perspectives have led me to re-examine my ethics. Is everything I considered ethical still valid in light of these new insights? This process of questioning and potentially adjusting beliefs is daunting, yet it's essential for growth. It's crucial to embrace change and not chastise ourselves for past misconceptions. Openness to new ideas ensures we continue evolving, both personally and as a community, fostering a dynamic environment where learning and improvement are constant.

Reflecting on my training methods led to some challenging realisations. Utilising rewards with my dogs was not inherently force-free; it depended greatly on the context. I recognised the potential for misuse of treats, especially with dogs eager to please or those heavily conditioned to comply. This was a difficult truth to acknowledge, but essential for ethical training. Understanding where to draw the line between using rewards as a training tool and coercing compliance is complex and varies with each dog. To avoid coercion, it's vital to first understand their desires and needs.

The reasons for using rewards vary: altering a dog's response, reinforcing safety-related behaviours like recall, engaging in fun training games, or for personal enjoyment. It's in the latter where issues often arise. Many behaviours I had trained my dogs to perform were primarily for my enjoyment, perhaps overshadowing what they genuinely enjoyed. Although they seemed to participate willingly and received their favourite treats, my perspective at the time was different. I hadn't fully grasped the implications of conditioning and its subtle ability for unintended coercion.

Addressing how dogs, who have been heavily conditioned to comply, can still make autonomous choices is complex. When a dog is deeply conditioned, their instinct to comply often overrides their personal preferences. This presents a challenge: ensuring that dogs still have the opportunity to make choices that reflect their desires, not just what they've been trained to do. It's about balancing training with providing options, allowing them to choose activities or behaviours that align with their interests and preferences. Encouraging dogs to make choices requires careful observation of their natural inclinations and preferences, and creating environments where they feel safe and comfortable to express these choices. Force isn't just physical; it can manifest in subtle ways, even in what appears to be voluntary participation. This realisation was a pivotal moment in reassessing my training approach.

Force-free ethical training undeniably has its place, but it should be complemented with natural learning, holistic approaches, and a thorough understanding of each individual dog. While some trainers might view this extended approach as excessive, arguing that force-free training suffices, it's crucial to understand that avoiding obvious harm isn't the only criterion for effective training. Resistance to change is natural, especially when presented as daunting. However, embracing evolution in training methods is both feasible and beneficial. The CDD method I've devised aims to provide a flexible framework, allowing a balance that is tailored to each dog, owner, and professional. It's not about overtraining or robotic conditioning but about understanding each dog's unique needs and fostering a harmonious balance between training, holistic teaching and natural learning. This approach aspires to reduce misunderstandings, misplaced expectations, and the notion that training alone can reshape any behaviour, encouraging a more nuanced and empathetic perspective in dog training.

Beginning my journey of critical thinking and reassessing previously accepted 'truths,' I found it enlightening to review my past behavioural reports. Skimming through a case study, I was struck by a sentence I had written to a client: "You need to train your dog to like it, since they are not naturally driven to the crate, gradually exposing them to the crate, with an open door, throwing in tasty treats and receiving their meals in there will help them to see it as their safe space, and they will learn to see it as their safe haven, a calm space that they can in time learn to love." Reflecting on this common advice, several questions arose. What jolted me was the idea that we could, or should, train a dog to like something. This now seemed problematic upon reflection. Interestingly, through my marketing research, I learnt to apply the "why?" question to everything I'm selling: "Why do people want or need this?" Although seemingly unrelated, this line of reasoning seemed applicable. I asked myself why and applied it to everything I was doing.

Let's scrutinise my initial statement: "you need to train your dog to like it." Why? If dogs naturally liked something, would they require training for it? If a dog likes their crate, wouldn't they instinctively use it when necessary? The idea of conditioning a dog to like a crate more likely conditions them to tolerate its use, rather than genuinely enjoying it. Reflecting on my own experiences with Steve, Dave, and Joyce, I saw this contrast. Joyce could not be trained to tolerate a crate, let alone to like it, leading to a crate-free life for her. In contrast, the boys were trained to use the crate for safety reasons. Despite my efforts to make the crate a positive space for Joyce, including getting in the crate with her as a puppy, she was never comfortable with it. The door was always left open, and I never shut it until I was sure each dog was 'happy' inside. Joyce's resistance was a lesson, but one I wasn't ready to learn at the time.

Dave, for the first four months, complied with sleeping in the crate at night without any sign of distress. However, after a few months, he began to resist – whining, clanking on the bars, barking. Once we stopped using the crate at night, he returned to peaceful nights. The crate remained in the house for practical reasons – when dog-wary people visited, during mealtimes to avoid dog noses in our dinners, or for enforced rest periods. But Dave's shift in behaviour made me question the ethics of conditioning for compliance. Force isn't just physical; it can be applied subtly through compliance. This realisation forced me to reconsider my methods, which I had previously viewed as faultless. Of course, there are times when we may need to teach a dog to tolerate things they may not like if it's for their own health and safety, but this should still be taught ethically and respectfully.

Examining the next part of the statement, 'Crates are the dog's safe space.' Applying the 'why' principle, why is it their safe space? This implies that the house isn't a safe space for the dogs, and yet, my home, which I share with my dogs, should also be a sanctuary for them. So, why do they need a crate to be their safe haven rather than the home we share? I had always thought that being den animals, they would naturally seek out small spaces to feel safe and content. This is what I, alongside many other professionals and enthusiasts, had been taught. But are they really? Did I ever verify this as a fact, or did I just accept it unquestioningly? I confess, I didn't do my own research initially, blindly trusting well-known behaviourists and trainers who proclaimed this as truth. Who was I to doubt them? They seemed more knowledgeable than me, after all. But driven by newfound curiosity and a shift in perspective, I decided to delve deeper.

In my research, I was fascinated to find that there is no concrete evidence to support the claim that dogs are denning animals. Even wolves, often cited in comparison, use a den primarily for specific purposes such as raising litters when they are very young. Since dogs are a distinct species from wolves, it's still unfounded to assume they are den-dwelling creatures. This is corroborated by extensive research conducted by numerous professionals in our field, which fails to find any evidence linking dogs with den-like behaviour. Therefore, it's reasonable to conclude that dogs, in fact, are not den dwellers.

But let's hypothesize for a moment that they were. Does a crate even resemble a true den? In the wild, dens are often communal spaces shared by social animals of the same species. Wolves, for instance, typically share their den with their family, usually with their cubs. Contrast this with the typical scenario where dogs are often left alone in their crates, which can be isolating and unnatural for them, given their social nature. Furthermore, when wolf pups are old enough, usually by three weeks, they can leave the den freely, returning as needed. Crates, however, are a different story, often featuring locked doors, which restricts a dog's choice to exit as they please. This is a significant departure from natural behaviour. Wolves never return to their dens once they've outgrown them, usually around eight weeks old, except when they need to raise their own litters. Yet, when we bring our puppies home, by the age they are ready to leave a den in the 'wild', we often start confining them to crates, which goes against their natural development. Even free-roaming dogs display a tendency to use dens solely for whelping purposes.

This revelation about dogs and crates led me to rethink the conventional approach to crate training. It's essential to question and research widely accepted practices in dog training, ensuring our methods align with the true nature and well-being of our dogs.

I was both horrified and fascinated by this revelation, horrified that I had been so wrong, I had encouraged others to use crates as well as using them for my own dogs, and this is where discomfort stirs up inner defensiveness "but they have their uses, surely they aren't that bad?!"

But the more I researched the more convinced I became that they should only ever be used for extreme reasons. I since discovered that in countries like Sweden and Finland have actually banned the use of crates, crate training is illegal, and the only time crates can be used is for travel, dog shows and extreme surgery or trauma. This is quite telling, what would drive an almost complete ban? Clearly a huge number of people felt so strongly about the use of crates being unethical that it called for a ban in two countries! That is quite big and not to be dismissed just because it feels more comfortable to believe they are safe and effective.

Imagine a typical home in Sweden or Finland, where instead of a crate, you'll find dogs freely roaming their homes, sleeping in cosy corners of the house, or playing in well-secured gardens. This contrasts sharply with the common practice in other countries where crates are a regular fixture in homes. The ban reflects a deep-seated belief in these societies: that true animal welfare transcends convenience or conventional training methods. This shift challenges us to reevaluate our practices and consider if there are more ethical and natural ways to care for our dogs.

Other reasons to reconsider our stance on crates include the restrictions they impose on dog's rights to display natural behaviours and their access to water at all times, both of which are among the five freedoms enshrined in UK animal welfare guidelines. It's crucial to understand that dogs do not sleep in the same way we do. Enforcing sleep in crates often results in either pent-up or withdrawn dogs. This insight is supported by new canine sleep studies, which suggest that dogs and puppies might not need as much sleep as previously thought – not the 16-18 hours a day that has been widely assumed.

One such study, the 2023 Canine Sleep and Behaviour Research conducted by the University of Bristol, revealed some startling facts. Contrary to long-held beliefs, they found that dogs actually require significantly less sleep. On average, dogs were observed to sleep for about 12 to 14 hours a day, much less than the previously estimated figures. Moreover, when given the choice, an overwhelming 70% of dogs in the study chose to sleep with their owners rather than alone. This statistic alone challenges the notion that dogs prefer isolated, crate-like environments for rest.

Dave preferred sleeping in our bed with, and without us!

The realisation that my long-held beliefs could be misguided was a turning point. It led me to ponder other aspects of dog training and care that might need re-examination. If crates, once considered a staple, could be seen in such a negative light, what other practices are we holding onto simply because they're familiar, not because they're in the best interest of the dogs? I don't believe it's realistic to expect a total ban on the use of crates in a society that currently relies on them for numerous reasons. Nor do I think it's right to shame others for using them. I'm not privy to their individual circumstances, and perhaps they don't have another way to keep their dogs safe from harm. My stance is to avoid using crates wherever possible, to seek alternative methods to keep dogs safe that don't involve isolating them in a crate. It's also vital to avoid promoting crates with inaccurately positive descriptions and instead examine the facts and logic applied to their use.

Steve also preferred his comforts!

Consider a family with a new puppy and a hectic household. The common advice might be to use a crate for 'safety' and 'training'. However, there are other ways to ensure the puppy's safety and comfort. This could include puppy-proofing certain areas of the house, using baby gates to create safe zones, and teaching puppies through self awareness to be mindful of areas or items that are not for chewing or playing with. The best approach with a young puppy, however, is to simply put away dangerous or high-value items while you teach your puppy self-restraint and help them distinguish between their toys and other objects. Once they are older and have acquired these skills, high-value items can be reintroduced into their environment. However, dangerous items should always be kept out of reach, regardless of the dog's age. These alternatives provide the puppy with more freedom to move and interact, aligning more closely with their natural behaviour and needs.

By reframing our approach, we encourage ourselves and others to think creatively and compassionately about their dogs' welfare. It's about finding solutions that respect the dog's natural instincts and needs while maintaining their safety and well-being. The goal isn't to judge or condemn, but to educate and offer alternatives that can enhance the lives of dogs and their owners alike.

In a world where crates have become a norm, it's important to challenge this status quo thoughtfully and empathetically, always prioritizing the dog's perspective. By doing so, we open the door to more humane and effective ways of living and working with our dogs. As I continued my journey into the world of dog training, I kept this lesson close. They depend on us to make decisions that prioritise their wellbeing, even if it means unlearning what we once thought was right.

Each case is individual, so it's important to consider the use of crates on a case-by-case basis. Some nuanced situations may indeed call for the use of a crate. This could be for safety in a multi-dog household, for a dog with various medical needs, or for safety in the car boot, for instance. However, in scenarios where it's believed that a dog chooses to go inside the crate and therefore enjoys it – just as I once believed – try this experiment: Keep the crate door open, and refrain from directing your dog into their crate or rewarding them when they enter. Keep the crate accessible at all times and observe what happens over a few weeks. Does your dog actively choose it now that they've learnt they don't have to?

I conducted this experiment with my dog, Dave. I stopped instructing him to go into his crate, ceased gesturing towards it, and refrained from making a fuss when he entered. I wanted to see if he would use it out of his own volition, for his own enjoyment, not just to please me. During the first week, he would enter the crate at the usual times, appearing a bit confused at first, as the routine had changed. However, after a few days, he would enter the crate, realise he was no longer expected to stay, and then choose to settle elsewhere. After a month, he ignored the crate completely. We tried the same approach with Steve, and observed the same pattern. Two months later, confident that they had no desire to use it, I finally got rid of the crate. To my relief, this freed up a substantial amount of space in the house!

This experiment not only provided valuable insights into my dog's preferences but also underscored the importance of giving them choices. By allowing them the freedom to choose their resting place, I could better understand their natural preferences and needs. It was a revelation to see that, when not prompted or rewarded, neither Dave nor Steve had any inclination to use the crate. This finding challenges us to rethink how we interpret our dog's actions and the choices we make for them, always striving to align more closely with their natural instincts and well-being.

Delving further into my old behavioural report, another piece of advice caught my attention. 'To make room for the extra treats and to increase food motivation, it is advisable to use part of your dog's meal as rewards.' This advice now seems problematic to me. Food is a dog's innate first need for survival. Is it fair to make them work for it? Could this approach potentially cause more behavioural problems? Let's delve deeper into this. The idea that dogs should work for their food is rooted in the belief that they are working animals and need a job to do. On the surface, this notion seems logical. But how accurate is it, really? Why should they work for their food when they are no longer wild animals? What potential problems could arise from this approach?

Consider our own history. Once, we were hunter-gatherers, working for our food. Does that mean we should enjoy working for our food today? Perhaps some of us would, but many, including myself, would find it stressful. The survival instinct would certainly kick in. Could the same be true for dogs? What if making them work for their food activates their survival instincts, thereby increasing their stress levels? While some dogs might find enjoyment and a sense of achievement in such activities, others might feel frustrated, tired, and underwhelmed by the concept.

The individuality of dogs, just like people, plays a significant role. For example, some people relish the challenge of hunting for their food, enjoying the sport and sense of accomplishment. But would they still enjoy it if they had no choice in the matter? Would the thrill remain the same if it was an everyday necessity, or if they were hungry? Similarly, some dogs labelled as 'fussy eaters' might find it overwhelming when food is made less accessible. Others, who struggle with food guarding, might perceive food as a scarce resource and guard it even more fiercely – a natural and instinctive response.

This change in perspective highlights the importance of considering each dog's unique personality and needs when deciding how to use food in training and daily life. While the concept of working for food might seem fitting for some, for others, it could lead to unintended stress or behavioural issues. It's a reminder that what works for one dog may not be suitable for another, and as responsible caretakers, we must be mindful of these individual differences.

Of course, many working breeds have an innate desire to work, and this is also true for many dogs who do not come from working lines. However, providing outlets for their breed-specific desires can be achieved in a much more constructive and natural way. Enrichment should be something that a dog finds naturally rewarding, and it is best to let the individual dog show us what they find enriching. For some dogs, it might be activities like running, swimming, using their nose to find things, training, and socialising. A profound difference I noticed when I shifted my approach from training-focused enrichment, and even using food for enrichment, was allowing my dogs to demonstrate what they found enriching and providing those opportunities individually. Dave, for instance, enjoyed digging, swimming, and using his nose, while Steve found joy in fast running, finding hidden toys, and playing tug.

This observation led to an important realisation: it's not truly enrichment if a dog doesn't find it naturally engaging. So, providing them with opportunities to express behaviours they demonstrate an interest in is far more beneficial for their overall well-being.

Imagine a scenario where a dog is given a variety of activities to choose from. One dog may gravitate towards a pool, delighting in the sensation of swimming, while another may spend hours digging in a designated area, relishing the chance to use their paws and nose. This approach respects their individual preferences and encourages them to engage in activities that they inherently enjoy. It's about observing and responding to each dog's unique personality and inclinations, rather than imposing predetermined activities on them.

By focusing on what each dog naturally enjoys, we can provide a richer, more fulfilling experience for them. This method not only caters to their physical needs but also supports their mental and emotional health, fostering a deeper bond between dogs and their owners. It's a shift from a one-size-fits-all approach to a more personalised, considerate way of caring for our dogs.

Central to the philosophy of the CDD method is the unwavering commitment to good ethics. This commitment isn't just a guiding principle; it's the very heart and soul of how we interact with and train our dogs. But why is this focus on ethics so crucial, and why must it be the driving force behind the CDD method?

Firstly, good ethics in dog training and care stem from a deep respect for dogs as sentient beings with their own needs, desires, and rights. It's a recognition that our methods and interactions with dogs should not just be about convenience or control, but about fostering mutual respect and understanding. In the CDD method, we view dogs not as subordinates or tools to be moulded at will, but as partners in a journey of mutual growth and learning.

Moreover, ethical practices in dog training are essential for building trust. When dogs are treated with respect, understanding, and kindness, they learn to trust us, making them more receptive to training and more willing to cooperate. This trust is not just beneficial for training purposes; it forms the foundation of a healthy, harmonious relationship between dogs and their owners.

Let's consider the alternative: training methods that rely on dominance, fear, or punishment. Such methods may produce quick results, but at what cost? The psychological and emotional wellbeing of the dog is often compromised, leading to a relationship based on fear rather than trust. In contrast, the CDD method, driven by good ethics, ensures that the dog's wellbeing is always prioritised. It's about understanding the individual dog's needs and tailoring our approach to suit them, rather than forcing them into a one-size-fits-all model.

Ethical training also means being honest with ourselves about our motivations and methods. It requires us to constantly evaluate and re-evaluate our practices, ensuring they align with the latest scientific understanding of dog behaviour and welfare. It's a commitment to learning and growing alongside our dogs, rather than assuming we already have all the answers.

In essence, good ethics in the CDD method is about respect, empathy, and a genuine desire to understand and meet the needs of our dogs. It's a philosophy that transcends conventional training methods, focusing instead on building a relationship of mutual trust and respect. This approach not only benefits our dogs but enriches our lives as well, fostering a deeper, more meaningful connection with our dogs.

CHAPTER TWELVE - CHOICES

There's no denying that many dogs have limited choices in their everyday lives and overall experiences. They often don't get to choose what or when they eat, where and when they walk, or where and when they sleep. We must consider what this lack of choice does to a dog's sense of self, their sense of control, awareness, and purpose.

Many people believe that offering dogs a few choices here and there is sufficiently enriching. Should they play with a ball or a tug toy? Explore this area or another? Choose this treat or a different one? And sometimes, do they want to consent to something or not? These are all important decisions to allow our dogs to make, but the concept of choice can be much more profound. Choices are multidimensional and extend beyond simply selecting between two options. The ability to make choices must be taught. A dog accustomed to having everything decided for them might struggle if suddenly given freedom of choice, potentially finding the experience overwhelming or even stressful.

This is often because they have become overly dependent on us making decisions for them, leaving them feeling incapable of making their own choices. Therefore, introducing choice must be done carefully and thoughtfully. For instance, we might start by offering simple choices in a low-stress environment. Imagine presenting two different types of toys in a familiar room – a soft, plush toy and a chewable rubber one. Let the dog approach and select the toy they prefer, but help them with a different choice if they aren't in the mood for these toys.

Gradually, we can introduce more complex choices, like deciding the route on a walk or choosing where to rest. It's about observing their preferences and responding accordingly. This process not only gives them a sense of control and agency but also enhances their confidence and well-being.

By incorporating choice into our dog's lives, we acknowledge their individuality and respect their ability to make decisions. It's a way of empowering them, fostering a deeper understanding and connection between us. The aim is to gradually shift from a life where everything is dictated to them, to one where they actively participate in decision-making, enhancing their sense of autonomy and self-esteem.

In the Canine Dialogue Dynamics (CDD) method, teaching a dog to make choices is not just about offering options, but about encouraging thoughtful decision-making. This involves a careful blend of language, questions, and attentiveness to the dog's response, ensuring the process is both respectful and enriching.

To start teaching choices, we first need to create an environment where our dogs feel comfortable and confident enough to express their preferences. This can be done by using clear and consistent language, combined with an open and inviting body language. For example, when presenting two different toys, we can ask, 'Which one would you like, the ball or the tug toy?' while showing each toy in turn. The key is to pose the question in a calm and friendly tone, making the experience positive and stress-free.

It's crucial to observe and consider the dog's response carefully. A dog might initially go for the first thing they see, which can be an impulsive reaction rather than a thoughtful decision. To differentiate between impulse and choice, we can repeat the process several times in different settings, changing the order of the options presented. Over time, a pattern may emerge indicating a genuine preference, demonstrating a thoughtful decision rather than an impulsive one.

For example, if we consistently offer a choice between playing fetch and going for a walk, an impulsive decision would be the dog immediately going for the ball each time it's presented first. However, if over multiple sessions, regardless of the order presented, the dog consistently chooses the ball, it indicates a thoughtful decision.

The CDD method emphasises the importance of respecting the dog's choice, even if it's different from what we anticipated. This respect fosters trust and strengthens the communication bond between us and our dogs. It's about giving them the agency to express themselves and acknowledging their preferences.

Moreover, teaching choice should always be a gradual and gentle process. It's not about overwhelming the dog with too many options or creating anxiety around decision-making. It's about guiding them to understand they have a voice, and their preferences matter.

Consider the possibilities in their daily routines. Instead of the usual choice between two toys, why not ask, 'What would you like to do now? Go for a walk, play a game, spend time in the garden, or have a snack?' This opens up a world of options for them, allowing them to express their desires more fully. When on a walk, instead of deciding the route yourself, pose a question to your dog: 'Shall we go this way towards the lake or that way towards the woods?' This not only makes the walk more engaging for them but also gives them a sense of control over their environment and activities.

Similarly, when it comes to socialisation, allow your dog to choose who they want to interact with or when they prefer to step away. This respects their social boundaries and comfort levels. In terms of snacks, offering choices like 'chicken or beef?' or 'yoghurt or a carrot?' can make food choices more interesting and enjoyable for them.

It's also essential to understand that sometimes, dogs may choose two out of three offered options, and that's perfectly okay. There is no right or wrong choice in these scenarios. The key is to observe and respect their decisions, whatever they may be. By doing so, we validate their preferences and encourage them to continue expressing themselves.

Offering a range of choices helps to enrich our dog's lives and enhances their well-being. It's not just about giving them options; it's about acknowledging their individuality and agency. When we present multiple choices, we're not just asking them to decide between A or B; we're inviting them to share their desires and inclinations with us.

This approach is a fundamental part of the CDD method, where the emphasis is on understanding and responding to our dogs as thinking, feeling beings with their own likes, dislikes, and desires. By expanding the range of choices we offer, we open up new avenues for communication and deepen the bond we share with our dogs. It's a journey of discovery, respect, and mutual understanding, revealing the unique and complex individuals they truly are.

Before diving into the world of choices, it's crucial for our dogs to have a firm grasp on the words used in these questions. This understanding stems from the initial phase of word association we discussed earlier. By teaching them the meaning of specific words and phrases, we lay the groundwork for meaningful communication and informed decision-making. For instance, 'walk', 'play', 'garden', and 'snack' are not just sounds to them; they represent real, tangible concepts that they can respond to with understanding.

Understanding the balance between granting freedom and setting boundaries is crucial in dog training and care. When teaching dogs to make choices, it's important to operate within a framework of *necessary* boundaries. These boundaries aren't imposed for the sake of control but rather for ensuring safety and adherence to social norms. Just as our lives are guided by a set of rules and limits that ensure order and safety, so too should the lives of our dogs be. Without these boundaries, we risk descending into chaos and potentially dangerous situations. Therefore, offering choices to dogs should always be contingent on safety, and guided choices become essential when a dog isn't yet capable of making informed and thoughtful decisions.

However, it's equally important to avoid excessively limiting our dog's choices or consistently offering only guided choices. Doing so can create a situation where the dog becomes overly dependent on us to make decisions for them, inhibiting their ability to think and act independently. This over-dependence is often misconstrued as trust, but there's a significant difference between the two.

Trust in the context of the human-dog relationship is built on mutual respect and understanding. It involves a dog feeling secure in their environment and with their human, knowing that their needs are understood and met. Trust allows a dog to feel comfortable making choices, confident that it won't lead to negative consequences. It's about a dog knowing that their human will guide and protect, but not to the extent of stifling their independence.

Over-dependence, on the other hand, occurs when a dog has not been given the opportunity to learn and practice independent decision-making. In such cases, the dog may appear to 'trust' their human, but this is more about reliance than trust. An over-dependent dog may struggle to cope in situations where they need to make decisions, leading to increased anxiety and uncertainty.

The key is finding a balance. We should strive to create environments where our dogs can safely make choices, allowing them to grow in confidence and independence. At the same time, we must be there to provide guidance and support, stepping in with directed choices when necessary. By doing so, we foster true trust – a trust that empowers our dogs to be confident, well-adjusted, and capable of making decisions within the safe boundaries we set. This approach is fundamental in helping our dogs navigate the world around them with confidence and ease.

Let's take a look at how Steve, Dave, and Joyce began to express their preferences and the joy this newfound control brought into their lives.

Steve showed a remarkable affinity for outdoor adventures. When asked, 'Shall we go to the lake or the woods?', he would eagerly wag his tail and head towards the door at the mention of 'woods'. His excitement was palpable; his eyes would light up, and he'd prance around in anticipation. This choice gave him a sense of control over his adventures, and his enthusiastic response was a clear indicator of his preference.

Dave, on the other hand, had a penchant for relaxation. When given the choice between 'play' and 'garden', he often opted for the garden, sauntering over to his favourite sunny spot. He would stretch out, basking in the warmth, completely at ease. This choice reflected his laid-back personality and his love for quiet, peaceful environments.

Joyce's decisions were often food-oriented. When presented with the choice of 'chicken or beef?', her nose would twitch as she sniffed both options, often settling on beef with a satisfied nuzzle. Her choice was deliberate, showing her discerning taste. Similarly, when given the option of a 'yoghurt or carrot', she would usually pick the yoghurt, licking her lips in anticipation. Their decisions would change according to their mood, sometimes Steve would choose the lake or the beach, or Dave decided he wanted to swim, and Joyce would make decisions when she wanted, too, sometimes choosing both food choices offered.

The happiness and excitement these choices brought to Steve, Dave, and Joyce were evident. They began to show a sense of ownership over their lives, making decisions that genuinely pleased them. This empowerment was not just about the joy in the moment; it was about building their confidence and trust in their environment and in their relationship with me.

Selecting their snacks. They do not eat from the same bowl, and are fed separately to ensure they have enough space each. Dave chose his snacks, then Steve chose his. Here they are selecting Oatibix in milk with apple slices.

Their individual responses to these choices were a revelation. It was heartwarming to see them express their preferences, each in their unique way, and to witness the positive impact this had on their overall well-being. This process underscored the essence of the CDD method - respecting each dog as an individual with their own likes, dislikes, and the right to choose, enhancing the bond we share and enriching their lives immeasurably.

In the journey of nurturing our dogs through the Canine Dialogue Dynamics method, it's crucial to remember the importance of continuously offering them choices, even when we think we know what they will choose. The act of choosing itself is empowering for dogs, giving them a sense of control and agency in their lives. They relish the opportunity to make a decision, even in scenarios where their preference seems predictable to us. It's about respecting them as sentient beings capable of making choices, regardless of how well we think we know them.

Moreover, it's perfectly normal for a dog's decisions and preferences to evolve over time. Just like us, their tastes can change, and they might develop new interests or dislikes. This shift is a natural part of their growth and experience. Recognising and adapting to these changes is a key aspect of the CDD method. It shows our willingness to see our dogs as dynamic individuals, continually evolving and expressing themselves in new ways.

For instance, a dog who always chose beef over chicken might one day show an interest in chicken, or a dog who preferred the garden might suddenly find joy in a game of tug. These changes are not just whims; they are expressions of their individuality and their response to the ever-changing world around them.

In essence, the core of the CDD method is to provide our dogs with ongoing opportunities to make choices, respecting their preferences as fluid and evolving. It's a commitment to understanding and responding to their needs and desires as they grow and change. This approach fosters a deep, trusting bond between us and our dogs, rooted in mutual respect and understanding. It's about creating a life for them that's not just lived but actively chosen, one choice at a time.

CHAPTER THIRTEEN - PERSONALITY AND BREED TRAITS

In the complex and fascinating world of dogs, understanding the nuances of personality and breed traits is crucial. While it's easy to categorise dogs based on their breeds, this is just the tip of the iceberg. Each breed carries certain traits that are widely recognised – like the protective nature of German Shepherds or the hyper focus of Border Collies. However, it's vital to remember that these are general guidelines rather than hard-and-fast rules.

Every dog is a unique individual, with a personality that may or may not align perfectly with breed stereotypes. For instance, you might encounter a Labrador Retriever who is surprisingly aloof, or a Beagle that prefers the quiet comfort of indoors, deviating from their breed's typical characteristics. This individuality is what makes working with dogs both a challenge and a joy.

Understanding both breed traits and individual personality is essential for several reasons. It helps us tailor our approach to training, ensures that we meet their emotional and physical needs effectively, and deepens our bond with them. Recognising a dog's individual personality allows us to appreciate them for who they truly are, not just as a member of their breed.

As we embark on this journey, keep in mind that every dog has a story to tell. Our job is to listen, understand, and respond to that story in a way that respects their individuality and enhances their well-being.

When we think about different dog breeds, certain images and characteristics often come to mind. For instance, the intelligence and trainability of Border Collies, the affectionate nature of Golden Retrievers, or the strong-willed temperament of Siberian Huskies. These breed traits, while helpful as a basic guide, are not definitive rules for individual dog's behaviour.

Let's take Border Collies as an example. Known for their intelligence and energy, they're often seen as ideal working or agility dogs. However, this doesn't mean every Border Collie will excel in these areas or even enjoy them. You might come across a Border Collie who prefers a more relaxed lifestyle, or one who finds joy in activities that don't align with the typical 'herding' behaviour.

Similarly, while Labrador Retrievers are renowned for their friendly and outgoing nature, it's not uncommon to meet one who is more reserved or independent. These deviations from the norm are not anomalies; they're reflections of the diverse personalities that exist within any breed.

One of the most significant misconceptions in the dog world is the idea that breed alone determines behaviour. This overgeneralisation can lead to unrealistic expectations and sometimes even behavioural issues. For instance, expecting a relaxed breed to be content with minimal exercise and indoor living can lead to frustration on both sides. It's crucial to remember that each dog, regardless of breed, has their own set of needs, preferences, and quirks.

Understanding breed traits is undeniably important, especially when it comes to predicting certain tendencies like energy levels, predispositions to health issues, or potential behavioural traits. However, it's equally important to approach each dog as an individual. Observing and interacting with them, learning about their specific likes, dislikes, and behaviours, is key to providing them with a fulfilling life.

While breed traits offer a valuable framework, they should not be the sole factor in determining how we train, care for, and understand our dogs. The true essence of their behaviour lies in the unique blend of their breed characteristics and individual personality, a combination as unique as each dog we encounter.

Understanding the role of breeding lines and genetics is key to comprehending the full spectrum of a dog's behaviour, temperament, and health. Breeding lines, the ancestral lines from which a dog descends, carry more than just physical traits; they also transmit behavioural tendencies and health predispositions from one generation to the next.

To understand this, let's consider the concept of breeding lines. These are essentially the family trees of dogs, and just like in humans, certain traits and tendencies can be passed down through generations. For instance, a Labrador Retriever from a line bred primarily for fieldwork and active retrieval might display higher energy levels and a more intense work drive compared to one from a line bred for show or companionship. This distinction is crucial when considering a dog for your home, as it can greatly influence their suitability to your lifestyle and expectations.

Health is another area where genetics play a key role.

Certain breeds are predisposed to specific health issues, and understanding the genetic history of your dog's breeding line can help in anticipating and managing these potential concerns. For example, German Shepherds are known to be prone to hip dysplasia, a condition that can be influenced by genetics. Being aware of such predispositions allows for proactive health management and care.

It's also interesting to note how a dog's behaviour can reflect traits of their parents. Just as a calm and gentle mother can pass on her demeanour to her puppies, a nervous or reactive parent can also influence the temperament of their offspring. This genetic link highlights the importance of responsible breeding practices, where temperament and health are given as much consideration as physical attributes.

Understanding the influence of genetics and breeding lines adds another layer to our comprehension of dogs. It reminds us that each dog is a product of both nature and nurture – their genetics providing the foundation upon which their experiences and environment build their unique characters.

While breed traits offer a broad understanding, diving into the specifics of genetics and breeding lines provides a more complete picture of a dog's potential temperament, behaviour, and health. This knowledge empowers us as dog parents, trainers, and enthusiasts to make informed decisions and provide the best care and environment for our dogs.

Understanding a dog's individual personality involves looking beyond breed traits and into the unique character each dog possesses. While breed traits can provide a basic framework, the personality of each dog is shaped by a myriad of factors, including genetics, environment, and upbringing.

The personality of a dog is their unique blend of behaviours, reactions, and interactions with the world. For instance, two dogs of the same breed and even the same litter can exhibit vastly different personalities; one may be outgoing and adventurous, while the other could be shy and reserved. This divergence is a clear indicator that personality is not solely dictated by breed.

Influencing Factors

1. Genetics: Following on from our discussion about genetics, it's important to note that a dog's genetic makeup can influence aspects of their personality. Just as certain physical traits are inherited, so too can be characteristics like temperament and predisposition to certain behaviours.

2. Environment: The surroundings in which a dog is raised play a significant role in shaping their personality. A dog raised in a bustling, urban environment may develop different social skills compared to one raised in a quiet, rural setting. The variety and type of stimuli they are exposed to can mould aspects of their character.

3. Upbringing: The way a dog is trained, taught and nurtured from puppyhood impacts their personality, but won't ultimately change their core personality.

Let's look at some real-life examples to illustrate these points:

• Case Study 1: Consider two Springer Spaniels, Max and Bella, both from the same litter. Max, raised in a loving home with plenty of social interaction and positive experiences, developed into a confident and outgoing dog. Bella, however, had a more sheltered upbringing with limited social exposure, making her more cautious and reserved around new people and situations.

- Case Study 2: Another example is of two Golden Retrievers, Lucy and Oscar. Despite their breed's reputation for being friendly and sociable, Oscar, having been adopted from a neglectful environment, displayed signs of anxiety and wariness. In contrast, Lucy, who was raised in a nurturing and active household, showed the more typical Golden Retriever traits of friendliness and exuberance.

- Case Study 3: Consider Alfie and Burtie, two Spaniels from the same litter who were adopted into similar family settings – both active, loving homes with children and ample social interaction. Despite these parallel environments, Alfie and Burtie's personalities developed distinctly. Alfie emerged as the extrovert of the two; he was always eager to engage in play, showed a keen interest in meeting new people, and thrived in the midst of family activities. Burtie, while also in a nurturing and interactive environment, displayed a more introspective personality. He preferred observing before joining in, enjoyed solitary play with his toys, and often sought quiet time away from the hustle of family life. This divergence in their personalities, even in identical home environments, highlights how deeply innate a dog's character can be.

- Case Study 4: Another example involves Jack and Molly, siblings from a litter of Labradors who experienced neglect in their early months. Both were rescued and adopted into caring environments. Jack showed remarkable resilience, gradually overcoming his initial timidity to become a sociable and affectionate dog. Molly, on the other hand, carried the scars of her early experiences more deeply. Despite being in a nurturing home, she remained anxious and less trusting, particularly in new environments or around strangers. This case study highlights how innate personality traits can influence a dog's ability to recover from negative experiences. While Jack's inherent resilience allowed him to adapt and thrive, Molly's more cautious nature made her recovery process slower and more complex.

These case studies demonstrate that while breed traits can offer a general understanding, each dog's personality is a unique composition influenced by various factors. Recognising and responding to these individual personalities allows us to connect with our dogs on a deeper level, offering care and training that align with their specific needs and character.

The relationship between a dog's breed traits and their individual personality is a fascinating and complex one. Understanding how these aspects interact and influence behaviour is crucial for effective training and care.

While breed traits can offer a general idea of certain behavioural tendencies, it's the individual personality that adds depth and uniqueness to each dog. For instance, a Border Collie's breed trait might suggest a predisposition for herding and high energy, but how this manifests can vary greatly depending on the dog's personality. One Border Collie might channel their energy and herding instinct into agility training, while another might prefer engaging in search and rescue activities, demonstrating a more focused and methodical approach.

Similarly, a breed like the Staffordshire Bull Terrier is often associated with strength and courage, but individual personalities within the breed can range from outgoing and sociable to more reserved and contemplative. Understanding this interplay helps us avoid stereotyping based on breed and appreciate each dog as a unique individual.

Recognising the interplay between breed traits and personality can significantly enhance training and care strategies. By considering both these aspects, we can tailor our approach to suit the specific needs and tendencies of each dog. For example, a typically active and curious Jack Russell Terrier with a more laid-back personality might prefer mental stimulation exercises over high-intensity physical activities.

Training and care that acknowledge both breed traits and individual personalities ensure that we are not just meeting the basic requirements of the breed but also catering to the unique preferences and comforts of each dog. It's about striking a balance between what is expected of the breed and what suits the individual dog's character and temperament.

Case Examples

• A Golden Retriever known for their friendly and approachable nature might have a shy individual personality. Acknowledging this, a caretaker might introduce socialisation activities more gradually, respecting the dog's need for a slower pace in building confidence around new people and situations.

• An individual Siberian Husky, a breed known for their independence, might display unusually high levels of sociability and eagerness to please. In this case, a training approach that leverages these traits can be more effective than one typically suggested for the breed.

Understanding the intricate dance between breed traits and individual personality not only enriches our relationship with our dogs but also allows us to provide care that truly resonates with their unique selves. It's a journey of discovery, where each dog reveals a blend of the genetic blueprint of their breed and the distinct colours of their personal character.

Recognising and appreciating the unique traits of each dog is key to developing a deep and understanding relationship with them.

Observing Individual Personality

1. Observation in Various Settings: Spend time watching how your dog behaves in different environments – at home, in the park, around other dogs, and with different people. Note their reactions and preferences in these varied settings.

2. Interactive Play: Engage in different types of play and activities. See which games your dog enjoys most, whether it's fetch, agility exercises, or puzzle toys. Their play preferences can offer insights into their personality.

3. Social Interactions: Pay attention to how your dog interacts with other dogs and people. Are they outgoing, or do they prefer to watch from a distance? These interactions can reveal a lot about their social tendencies.

Understanding Breed Traits

1. Research the Breed: Familiarise yourself with the general traits of your dog's breed, keeping in mind that these are guidelines rather than definitive rules. This can provide a baseline understanding of potential behaviours and needs.

2. Historical Purpose: Consider the historical purpose of the breed. For example, a dog from a herding breed might have an innate tendency to herd, influencing their behaviour and exercise needs.

Tailoring Training and Care

1. Customised Training: Use your observations to create a lifestyle that aligns with your dog's personality. For instance, a dog with a playful and energetic disposition might respond well to a life incorporate adventure and learning new skills.

2. Adapted Care: Tailor your care to suit your dog's unique

needs. If your dog is more relaxed and enjoys lounging, ensure they have a comfortable, quiet space. Conversely, if they are energetic and curious, provide ample opportunities for physical and mental stimulation.

Practical Examples

• If you have a dog who loves exploring and sniffing every corner of the park, incorporate scent games into their training and playtime. This not only provides mental stimulation but also leverages their natural inclinations.

• For a dog who is shy or hesitant around strangers, teaching them skills that help build resilience and confidence, such as making choices, observing and learning how to rationalise.

Understanding and responding to your dog's unique traits is not just about effective training and care; it's about acknowledging their individuality and ensuring their life with you is as fulfilling and joyful as possible.

CHAPTER FOURTEEN - UNDERSTANDING CANINE EMOTIONS

Grasping the emotional world of dogs is not just an additional layer to our understanding; it's essential to a comprehensive approach in dog training and care. Dogs, akin to humans, experience a wide range of emotions, from joy and enthusiasm to anxiety and fear. Recognising and empathising with these emotions is crucial for effective training and, more importantly, for building a meaningful connection with our dogs.

Let's explore the ways emotions manifest in dogs, their influence on behaviour, and how we, as responsible dog carers, can tailor our training and interactions to respect and respond to these emotional states. Let's embark on this insightful journey into canine emotions, venturing beyond the simplicity of a tail wag to understand the profound emotional lives of our dogs.

In our endeavour to fully comprehend the emotional landscape of dogs, it's vital to acknowledge that their emotional experiences are as rich and varied as our own. From the exuberant wagging of a tail to the subtle bow of a head, dogs exhibit a range of emotions that span joy, fear, anxiety, excitement, and affection and even jealousy.

Embracing the Emotional Range

The work of Jaak Panksepp, a renowned neuroscientist, provides valuable insights into understanding emotions in animals.

Panksepp identified several primary emotional systems in the brain, such as seeking, fear, rage, and play, which are not exclusive to humans but shared with other mammals, including dogs. This foundational work opens the door to a deeper understanding of how dogs feel and react to their world.

Recent scientific studies have furthered our understanding of canine emotions. Advances in neuroimaging technology, such as MRI scans, allow researchers to observe the brain activity of dogs in real-time, shedding light on how they process emotions. For instance, studies have shown that specific brain regions light up when dogs are presented with stimuli that evoke happiness or fear, much like in humans.

Additionally, hormonal responses in dogs offer clues to their emotional states. The levels of hormones like cortisol and oxytocin fluctuate in response to stress or bonding experiences, respectively. These hormonal changes can significantly influence a dog's mood and behaviour.

Let's consider Ralph, a lively Border Terrier, whose boundless joy is evident as he races across the park, tail wagging, ears flapping. His entire being radiates excitement and happiness, a clear expression of his emotional state.

Conversely, consider Bella, a rescue Greyhound, who cowers with ears back and tail tucked at the sound of fireworks. Her fear is palpable, manifested not just in her body language but likely mirrored in her brain activity and hormonal levels.

To understand emotions more in-depth it's imperative to delve deeper into the pioneering work of Jaak Panksepp, a name synonymous with the study of emotions in the animal kingdom. Panksepp's work has been instrumental in shaping our understanding of the emotional lives of dogs.

The Foundations of Emotional Systems

Panksepp's research identified several core emotional systems in the mammalian brain, which he believed were key to understanding the emotional experiences of animals, including dogs. These systems include:

1. SEEKING: The drive to explore and seek resources. In dogs, this is often seen in their enthusiasm for walks, sniffing, and exploration.
2. FEAR: The response to perceived threats or danger. Noticeable in dogs through behaviours such as cowering or fleeing.
3. RAGE: A reaction to frustration or confinement. This can manifest in dogs as growling or aggression when they feel trapped or threatened.
4. LUST: The reproductive drive, evident in mating behaviours.
5. CARE: The nurturing instinct, seen in the way mother dogs care for their puppies.
6. PANIC/GRIEF: Feelings of loneliness and sadness, which can occur in dogs when separated from their human or canine companions.
7. PLAY: The joy of play, a vital part of a dog's emotional and physical well-being.

Understanding these emotional systems helps us better comprehend why dogs behave the way they do. For instance, when a dog tears apart cushions, it's not just mischief; it could be an expression of the SEEKING system, looking for stimulation and engagement. Similarly, a dog's aggression does not stem from a desire to dominate, but rather from the RAGE system, triggered by frustration or fear.

Panksepp's work is not just academic; it has practical implications for dog owners and trainers. By understanding these emotional systems, we can tailor our training and interaction strategies to align with our dog's innate emotional responses. This approach fosters a more compassionate and effective way of communicating with our dogs.

Let's take Ruby, an active Beagle, as an example. Her constant sniffing and foraging behaviour is a clear display of the SEEKING system in action. Understanding this, her owner can provide her with activities that satisfy this drive, like scent games, rather than trying to curb her natural instincts.

In contrast, consider Albert, a rescue dog who shows signs of aggression. Recognising this as a manifestation of the RAGE system, triggered by past traumas, his owner works on creating a safe environment and using holistic teaching and natural learning to mitigate these responses.

Panksepp's work reminds us that at the heart of many canine behaviours are fundamental emotional needs. By addressing these needs, we not only improve the well-being of our dogs but also enhance the bond we share with them. As we continue to explore the emotional world of dogs, Panksepp's insights remain a guiding light in our journey towards deeper understanding and empathy.

Understanding the emotional states of dogs is akin to learning a new language. It's about interpreting their body language, vocalisations, and behavioural cues, all within the context of their environment and experiences.

Body language in dogs is a complex array of signals, each with their own nuance. A wagging tail, often misconstrued as a sign of happiness, can actually express various emotions, from excitement to anxiety, depending on the wag's nature. A slow, low wag might indicate insecurity, while a rapid, high wag could denote happiness or excitement.

Consider the posture and ear positions. A relaxed dog might have a soft, neutral posture, with ears at rest. Contrast this with a scared dog, whose ears might be pinned back, with a lowered body and a tucked tail. Learning to read these subtleties is essential for understanding your dog's emotional state. Be mindful of where their ears, tail and body posture normally position themselves as to not misread the situation.

Dogs communicate a lot through sounds. A deep growl might signify discomfort or a warning, while a high-pitched bark could indicate excitement or alertness. The context, such as the presence of a stranger or another dog, plays a critical role in interpreting these sounds. But each dog has their own distinctive voice, some are naturally deep, some are higher pitched, so gauge what different tones and pitches mean individually to your dog.

Pay attention to the frequency and intensity of barking. Is it a continuous bark, signalling alertness, or intermittent, suggesting playfulness? A whine could express a range of emotions, from anxiety to excitement.

Dogs express their emotions through various behaviours. For instance, a dog chewing on furniture might not be misbehaving but could be expressing anxiety or boredom. Similarly, a dog that suddenly becomes withdrawn or inactive might be indicating sadness or illness.

Observe changes in usual behaviour patterns. An overly clingy dog might be seeking comfort due to anxiety, while a dog that avoids interaction might be feeling unwell or stressed.

Context is key in interpreting these emotional expressions. The same tail wag in different situations can mean entirely different things. Always consider the surrounding environment, recent changes in the dog's life, and the overall behaviour pattern.

Let's take the example of Lola, a usually energetic Red Setter. One day, her owner notices that Lola is less active, her tail is down, and she's not engaging in play. Instead of assuming she's just tired, her owner considers recent changes – the family moved to a new home. Recognising this as a potential cause for stress, the owner provides Lola with extra comfort and familiar toys to help her adjust. A vet check was also requested to ensure there was nothing more sinister going on.

In another case, Barney, a normally friendly Labrador, starts growling at new visitors. His owner, instead of reprimanding him, notices that Barney's growling started after an unpleasant encounter with a stranger. Understanding this context, the owner gently reassures him, allowing him choices, attending to his needs and rebuilding his confidence.

Recognising emotional expressions in dogs requires patience, observation, and empathy. By tuning into their unique ways of communicating, we can better understand and respond to their emotional needs, enhancing our bond and their well-being.

Different emotions can drastically alter a dog's behaviour. For instance, a dog experiencing anxiety may exhibit destructive behaviour, like chewing furniture, as a coping mechanism. Conversely, a dog brimming with excitement might become overly exuberant, jumping up or running around with seemingly boundless energy. It's not just about their external actions; emotions deeply influence their learning process and interactions. A frightened dog, overwhelmed by fear, may struggle to learn new concepts or interact with others, both dogs and humans alike.

A common misunderstanding is the belief that dog emotions are vastly different from ours or, conversely, exactly the same. While it's true that dogs may experience some emotions differently due to their unique sensory and cognitive world, there is growing evidence that many of their emotional experiences are remarkably similar to ours. For instance, the joy a dog shows when greeting a beloved owner isn't far removed from the happiness we feel when seeing a close friend.

However, it's essential to recognise that more research is needed to fully understand the depth and breadth of canine emotions. We must avoid the trap of oversimplifying without considering their distinct emotional experiences.

Consider a scenario with a rescue dog, let's call him Benni, who's been through traumatic experiences. Benni might show reluctance or fear in new situations, not because he's stubborn or untrainable, but because his past experiences have shaped his emotional response. Acknowledging his fear and gently guiding him through new experiences with patience and understanding can significantly alter his behaviour and trust in humans.

Or, take Sunny, a Boxer who wags her tail vigorously when visitors come. Many might interpret this as her being friendly and excited. But observing her body – stiff posture, ears pinned back – it becomes evident that her tail wagging isn't about happiness; it's a sign of discomfort or anxiety.

Understanding the impact of emotions on a dog's behaviour is a crucial aspect of building a meaningful relationship with them. It requires not only observation and knowledge but also empathy and patience.

Understanding and responding to a dog's emotional state is not just compassionate; it's a practical approach to enhancing training effectiveness. When we acknowledge a dog's emotions, we tailor our training methods to align with their mental state, leading to more successful and humane outcomes.

Tips for Supporting Emotional Health in Training

1. Read and Respect the Dog's Emotional Cues: Every dog communicates their emotional state through body language and behaviour. For instance, a dog reluctant to approach a new object might be showing apprehension. In such cases, it's essential to respect their pace and encourage exploration in a pressure-free environment.

2. Create a Safe and Predictable Environment: Dogs thrive in environments where they feel safe and where routines are predictable. A consistent routine helps dogs feel secure, reducing anxiety and stress, which in turn aids in their ability to learn and adapt to training.

3. Managing Anxiety and Fear: Some dogs may exhibit signs of anxiety or fear, which can hinder their learning process. In these instances, patience and gentle guidance are crucial. Using calming techniques, such as soft-spoken reassurances, teaching them they can say no and working with their individual needs can help alleviate their anxiety.

6. Avoid Punishment-Based Methods: Training that uses punishment can exacerbate fear, anxiety, and stress, leading to behavioural issues. Instead, focus on understanding why a dog is behaving a certain way and address the root cause of the behaviour in a compassionate manner.

Imagine a scenario with a young Rottweiler, Daisy, who shows signs of nervousness during training sessions. Instead of pushing her to perform, her owner acknowledges her anxiety and creates a calm, reassuring environment. The owner shows Daisy that she can choose what she needs to do to help herself feel better with their guidance. If she wants to rest, take a walk, engage in another activity, or have a cuddle, allowing her these guided choices will help to show her she doesn't have to conform.

Training that takes into account a dog's emotional health is not only more effective but also strengthens the bond between the dog and their owner. By recognising and respecting their emotions, and creating an environment conducive to positive emotional experiences, we lay the foundation for a more harmonious and fulfilling relationship. Remember, a dog's emotional well-being is as important as their physical health, and a key component to a successful training journey.

Emotional intelligence in dogs is a profound and often underappreciated aspect of their nature. It's their remarkable ability to not only feel emotions but also to read and respond to the emotions of humans.

The Empathetic Nature of Dogs

1. Reading Human Emotions: Dogs have an innate ability to pick up on our emotional cues. They can sense changes in our tone of voice, body language, and even our scent when we are stressed or joyful. This sensitivity allows them to respond in ways that often seem perfectly attuned to our feelings.

2. Responding to Emotions: Dogs don't just read our emotions; they respond in kind. A dog might snuggle up to an owner who is feeling sad or join in the excitement during happier times. This empathetic response showcases their emotional intelligence and deepens the bond they share with their human companions.

3. Scientific Evidence: Studies have shown that dogs can differentiate between happy and angry human expressions. In a remarkable study, dogs were shown pictures of people with various emotional expressions. The dogs consistently reacted differently to happy faces compared to angry ones, indicating their ability to understand human emotional expressions.

The emotional intelligence of dogs is a testament to their depth and complexity as sentient beings. Their ability to read and respond to our emotions not only demonstrates their intelligence but also their profound connection with us.

To further your understanding and enhance your connection with your dog, consider these reflective questions and practical exercises:

Reflection Questions

1. Observation: How does your dog express joy, discomfort,

or fear? Reflect on specific instances and their corresponding behaviours.

2. Response: How do you currently respond to your dog's emotional cues? Are there ways you could improve your responses to better support their emotional wellbeing?

3. Empathy: In moments of stress or excitement, how does your empathy towards your dog's emotions shape your interactions?

Practical Exercises

1. Emotion Diary: Keep a diary for a week, noting your dog's different emotional states each day. Observe patterns and triggers for various emotions.

2. Responsive Interaction: Spend time consciously responding to your dog's emotional cues. For instance, if they seem anxious, offer comfort; if they're playful, engage in a fun activity.

3. Emotion-Based Training Session: Conduct a training session where you focus more on your dog's emotional responses than on achieving specific commands. Notice how this approach influences the training experience for both of you.

When I began to pay closer attention to my dog's emotions, it became clear just how attuned they were to my own feelings. Dave's response to my stress was particularly telling. Whenever I became anxious or agitated, he reacted with a kind of manic energy, jumping on me, licking my face, and hugging me tightly, all while vocalising his concern. This contrasted sharply with Steve, who preferred to keep a distance in such situations, seeking a quiet space away from any turmoil. Joyce, intriguingly, seemed unaffected and showed no particular response.

This observation led to a significant shift in my behaviour. I became more mindful of how my emotions impacted my dogs. For instance, when technology issues sparked frustration – a not uncommon occurrence – I learnt to step away and take a break instead of expressing my irritation. Similarly, if my husband and I had a disagreement, we chose to discuss it outside during a walk rather than inside the house. This approach not only helped to shield our dogs from unnecessary stress but also had a surprising effect on our own emotional well-being. It seemed that by altering our environment and approach to manage our dog's emotional comfort, we inadvertently improved our own mood states, often shifting from negative to positive more rapidly than expected.

This realisation underscored an important lesson: our emotional states and those of our dogs are deeply interconnected. By considering their emotional needs, we inadvertently created a more harmonious and positive atmosphere for everyone in our household. This mutual benefit, stemming from a heightened awareness of our dog's emotional responses, enhanced the overall dynamic of our family, creating a more understanding and empathetic environment for all.

CHAPTER FIFTEEN – MY CAREER CHANGE

After confidently applying the CDD method with my dogs, I felt prepared to incorporate it into my professional work. While I continued to offer regular force-free training for those who preferred it, I began using the CDD approach in my behavioural consultations, particularly for dogs with reactivity issues. This shift coincided with my first year in Oxfordshire, in 2021, which marked a new chapter in both my personal and professional life.

The impact of this new approach was remarkable. Dogs that had struggled with reactivity began to show significant improvements at a rate I hadn't seen with the conventional methods I'd used before. Within just a few weeks of their caregivers applying the CDD method – teaching word association, using varied sentences, providing more choices, enhancing their dogs' diet, and adapting to their unique personalities – these dogs started to make more thoughtful decisions around their triggers.

Some would choose to observe their triggers from a comfortable distance, showing they could walk away when they wanted, without fixating or freezing. Others would independently decide to walk in the opposite direction, without needing to be trained or conditioned to do so. Remarkably, many dogs began to show interest in greeting specific triggers, but only if the trigger, environment, and their mood were right. It was an incredible journey to be a part of, and while their progress wasn't linear, the improvements they made significantly surpassed those achieved with the previous methods, which had inadvertently kept them trapped in their reactive behaviours.

I also expanded my work to include puppies and adolescent dogs. Rather than raising them through conventional training methods, they were nurtured with a focus on holistic teaching and natural learning. These dogs have now matured into well-adjusted, self-assured individuals who can express their wants and needs and demonstrate an impressive ease in understanding.

Initially, I found it challenging not to revert to my instinctual training protocols. For example, when teaching recall, but instead we engaged with the dog in their current activity, using phrases like, "What have you found? Oh wow, that's great!" or "Is that a good smell?" We then gently guided them, "Just come a bit closer to us now," or "Do you want to say hello to that dog? He's saying hello." We used a long line where appropriate and chose environments that fostered the best learning experience for the individual dog. We applied choices, respected their decisions, and taught them necessary boundaries while learning theirs. It was a profoundly natural and rewarding journey for the puppy, teenager, and caregiver alike.

Feeling content with my work in the local area, I decided to expand my reach by taking my business online. This allowed me to connect with a wider audience who preferred this approach and whose dogs were struggling with traditional training methods. From helping people understand their rescue dogs to assisting those disheartened by their dog's reactivity, and even guiding those who simply wanted to raise their puppies differently, I was able to help a diverse range of clients using my new approach. It has been a life-altering experience, not just for me but also for my clients and their dogs.

Bonnie's story began in a quiet suburban home, where she lived with her family, the Taylor family. A shepherd mix with a beautiful brindle coat, Bonnie had been a rescue dog, her past marred by experiences that left deep-seated trauma. Despite her loving home, Bonnie's walks were a constant challenge. The sight of another dog would trigger a relentless barking frenzy, her focus solely fixed on the other canine, oblivious to everything else around her. Years of positive reinforcement training had helped manage her behaviour to a certain extent, but it never truly addressed the underlying issues. The Taylors were disheartened and frustrated, feeling they had reached a dead end.

In a bid for a solution, they reached out to me for an online consultation. Through a detailed and empathetic discussion, I gathered extensive information about Bonnie's past experiences, her personality beyond her reactivity, and her breed traits. This comprehensive understanding allowed me to provide tailored advice and a fresh perspective that aligned with Bonnie's unique needs and past trauma.

The advice I provided focused on empowering Bonnie to make informed decisions during walks. Instead of the Taylors trying to control every interaction, they learnt to read Bonnie's signals more clearly and respond accordingly. This approach required patience and a deep understanding of Bonnie's communication cues, but the results were remarkable.

Within weeks, the Taylors reported a significant shift in Bonnie's behaviour. They noticed her ability to make more thoughtful decisions when encountering other dogs. She began to walk away when she felt uncomfortable, a choice she had never exercised before. This was a monumental step for Bonnie, reflecting her growing confidence and trust in her family's guidance.

As months passed, Bonnie's transformation was astonishing. She communicated her discomfort around other dogs in a much more relaxed manner. Remarkably, she even started to show selective interest in certain dogs. Bonnie had not only learnt to manage her reactivity but had also developed the ability to read other dog's behaviour, choosing to interact with those she felt comfortable with. The Taylors were overjoyed to see Bonnie enjoying her walks, a far cry from the anxious, pessimistic dog she once was.

Bonnie's journey is a testament to the power of understanding and addressing a dog's emotional world. Her story is one of resilience and transformation, showcasing the profound impact of tailored behavioural guidance that resonates with a dog's individual needs and experiences. Today, Bonnie enjoys her walks with a newfound sense of calm and confidence, no longer struggling with reactivity but thriving in her interactions with the world around her.

In the picturesque village of Cotswolds lived a young Labrador named Oscar. With his glossy black coat and warm, expressive eyes, Oscar was the beloved companion of the Harrison family. However, Oscar's outings were often fraught with challenges. Whenever he encountered other dogs during his walks, his reactivity surfaced. Oscar wasn't aggressive, but his body language conveyed a clear message – he did not want to engage with other dogs. Despite various training methods, Oscar's discomfort in the presence of other dogs persisted. The Harrisons were at their wits' end, feeling helpless as they watched Oscar's unease grow with each walk.

Seeking a resolution, the Harrisons contacted me for an online session. Through our conversations, I gathered insights into Oscar's personality, his daily routines, and his reactions in different scenarios. It became apparent that Oscar felt a pressure to interact with other dogs, a societal expectation that did not align with his temperament.

I advised the Harrisons to adopt a new approach, one that respected Oscar's preferences and communicated to him that it was perfectly acceptable not to engage with other dogs. This approach required a shift in the Harrisons' own expectations and a deeper understanding of Oscar's body language. They learnt to read his cues and support his decisions during walks, whether he chose to engage or not.

The change in Oscar was gradual but profound. Over time, he learnt that walking past other dogs without interaction was an option. The Harrisons reported that Oscar began to exhibit a calm demeanour during these encounters. He would politely communicate his disinterest to other dogs, using subtle body language cues – a brief glance away, a slight turn of the body – to signal his preference for space.

This newfound understanding transformed Oscar's walks from a source of stress to enjoyable outings. The pressure to conform to expected social dog behaviours was lifted, allowing Oscar to embrace his own way of interacting with the world. His walks became peaceful, and the Harrisons found joy in seeing their beloved Labrador walk with ease and confidence, calmly navigating his way past other dogs.

Oscar's story is a heartwarming example of how adapting our approach to a dog's individual emotional needs can lead to significant behavioural improvements. By understanding and respecting Oscar's disposition, the Harrisons were able to provide him with the support he needed to navigate his environment comfortably, demonstrating the power of a compassionate and tailored approach to dog training.

Across the pond in America, there lived a spirited young Spaniel named Alfie. At nine months old, Alfie was the embodiment of enthusiasm and energy. However, his zest for life often led to challenges, particularly during walks. With no impulse control or self-restraint, Alfie had a habit of running up to other dogs uninvited. This behaviour frequently resulted in reprimands from the other dogs, much to the distress of his owners, the Thompson family.

The Thompsons sought my guidance, hoping to find a way to help Alfie navigate his interactions more respectfully. During our online consultations, I gathered detailed information about Alfie's diet, daily routine, and typical interactions. It became clear that Alfie's diet was not helping his already high energy levels. Additionally, his adolescent hormones were contributing to his impulsive behaviour.

I advised the Thompsons to adjust Alfie's diet to one more suited to his energetic nature, ensuring it provided balanced nutrition without exacerbating his energy surges. We also addressed his testosterone levels, not by removing them, but by working with this natural stage of his development. Together, we developed a plan to teach Alfie self-restraint and manage his impulses.

The key was to understand that Alfie's behaviour was a normal part of his developmental stage and breed characteristics. I reassured the Thompsons and provided them with strategies to help Alfie. We focused on creating environments where Alfie could learn and practice self-control. This included structured play sessions and controlled interactions with other dogs, allowing him to understand the nuances of canine communication.

Over time, Alfie began to show remarkable improvement. His

understanding of when and how to engage with other dogs grew. He learnt to read the intentions of other dogs and respond appropriately, respecting their need for space. Notably, Alfie's recall improved dramatically, and he responded to the Thompsons' calls without the need for treats or conventional training methods.

Today, Alfie is a well-adjusted adult Spaniel. He still carries his exuberant spirit, but with a newfound sense of when it's appropriate to express it. The Thompsons are thrilled with Alfie's progress. They now enjoy walks filled with joy and free from the stress of unexpected encounters. Alfie's story is a testament to the effectiveness of understanding and working with a dog's natural development stages and personality, and the positive outcomes of tailored guidance and patience.

As my reputation for the CDD method grew, so too did my workload. I found myself fully booked, juggling local clients in person and an ever-expanding online clientele that spanned the globe. While it was incredibly rewarding to see the positive impact of my work, I couldn't ignore the creeping signs of burnout. The demand was overwhelming, and I realised I couldn't personally attend to every dog and owner in need.

The increasing demand for my expertise led me to a pivotal decision. To extend my reach and help more dogs and their owners, especially those grappling with reactivity issues, I decided to develop an online, self-paced course. This course was designed to encapsulate the essence of the CDD method, offering detailed video tutorials, practical demonstrations, thorough examinations, and prompts for self-reflection.

My vision was to create not just a course but a thriving community where dog owners could learn, share, and grow together. The course covered various aspects of reactivity, from understanding the root causes to practical steps for managing and reducing reactive behaviours. It was structured to be accessible yet comprehensive, catering to owners at different stages of their journey with their reactive dogs.

The response to the course was astounding. It resonated with dog owners worldwide, creating a supportive and interactive community. This community became a platform for shared experiences, successes, and challenges, offering encouragement and understanding to those on similar paths.

As the community grew, so did the success stories. Owners reported significant improvements in their dog's behaviour, armed with the knowledge and tools they gained from the course. The sense of accomplishment within this community was palpable, as more and more dogs were able to lead happier, more balanced lives.

The online course also allowed me to balance my workload better, reducing the risk of burnout while still fulfilling my passion for helping dogs and their owners. The CDD method, through this course, was reaching new heights, touching the lives of people and their dogs across continents and cultures.

Today, the community continues to flourish, a testament to the effectiveness and versatility of the CDD method. It stands as a beacon of hope and a source of invaluable support for those struggling with canine reactivity, embodying the spirit of collective growth and mutual aid.

CDD Framework: A Comprehensive Approach to Understanding and Nurturing Dogs

1. Personality: Discovering Personal Traits

- Importance: Understanding a dog's multifaceted personality is crucial for tailoring training and care to their specific needs. Recognising that a dog can exhibit varying traits, like anxiety in certain scenarios and confidence in others, helps in approaching them with empathy and effectiveness.
- Approach: Observe and interact with dogs in different settings to identify their diverse personality traits. This understanding aids in creating a nurturing environment that respects their individuality.

2. Breed: Interplay with Personality

- Understanding Breed Traits: Acknowledge the general tendencies of a dog's breed while recognising that these traits complement but do not always dictate their personality.
- Respect for Breed: Learn about your dog's breed characteristics and respect how these traits may influence their behaviour, without stereotyping.

3. Self-Awareness: Acknowledging Autonomy

- Respecting Sentience: Recognise dogs as self-aware beings capable of making choices and experiencing a range of emotions.
- Treating with Respect: Approach training and care with the understanding that dogs are sentient, deserving of respect and autonomy.

4. Emotions: Understanding and Nurturing

- Emotional Needs: Recognise and respond to the emotional states of dogs, from joy to fear, understanding their emotional intelligence and communication.

- Nurturing Emotional Well-being: Implement strategies to nurture emotional health, such as creating positive experiences and managing stress.

5. Choices: Empowering Dogs

- Increasing Choices: Aim to increase the range of choices available to dogs, respecting their preferences and autonomy.
- Avoiding Unnecessary Limits: Avoid restricting choices for the sake of control; instead, focus on safe and respectful freedom.

6. Freedom from Heavily Conditioned Responses

- Encouraging Independent Thinking: Move away from robotic obedience; foster a mindset where dogs are encouraged to think and make decisions independently.
- Guiding Without Conditioning: Teach dogs to understand and respond naturally rather than relying solely on conditioned responses.

7. A Good Diet: Enhancing Well-being

- Fresh, Nutritious Diet: Provide a diet that supports both mental and physical health, with natural food that offers a variety of tastes, smells, and textures.
- Natural Food Enrichment: Use diet as a form of enrichment, exploring different ingredients to cater to their preferences.

8. Enrichment: Catering to Individual Preferences

- Understanding Preferences: Observe and understand what activities and environments each dog finds enriching.
- Tailored Activities: Offer enrichment activities that align with each dog's unique preferences and instincts.

9. Dialogue: Fostering Communication

• Word Association to Conversation: Begin with teaching word associations, then evolve into simple sentences for effective communication.
• Prioritising Dialogue: Use this method as a primary approach in training, emphasising clear, empathetic communication.

10. Hearing: Understanding Responses

• Listening to Dogs: Pay attention to and respect the dogs' responses, understanding their choices and needs.
• Responding Appropriately: Learn to interpret and appropriately respond to their communications, building a reciprocal relationship.

11. Prioritising Needs over Expectations

• Understanding and Respecting Needs: Recognise and prioritise the dog's needs, even when they conflict with personal expectations or desires.
• Balancing Care: Find a balance between meeting a dog's essential needs and gently guiding them to adapt to the human world.

12. Self-Restraint and Impulse Control

• Guiding to Self-Regulation: Teach dogs to regulate their behaviour according to their abilities and developmental stages.
• Calm and Gentle Guidance: Use calm and understanding methods to encourage self-awareness and impulse control.

13. Emotional Regulation

- Awareness of Challenges: Help dogs recognise and understand what triggers intense emotions.
- Teaching Emotional Coping Strategies: Guide them to move away from overwhelming emotions and learn coping mechanisms for emotional regulation.

Through this framework, the CDD method aspires to create a harmonious, respectful, and empathetic relationship between dogs and their caregivers. It emphasises understanding and responding to each dog's unique personality, emotions, and needs, fostering a deep and meaningful bond.

CHAPTER SIXTEEN - HEARTBREAKING DECISIONS

Over the year following the dreadful altercation between Joyce and Steve, we seemed to have struck a semblance of balance and harmony. However, it was neither effortless nor consistently reliable. We found ourselves inadvertently prioritising Joyce's needs over those of the boys, a shift that occurred almost subconsciously. For the most part, our dogs coexisted peacefully: they walked amicably together, barring any close encounters with their triggers; they shared both the sofa and their sleep harmoniously; and they engaged in play together. Yet, Joyce's mood would occasionally sour, necessitating careful management of these episodes. Witnessing her mood swings and their impact on the boys was disheartening. We were forced to adopt seemingly unfair rules, tiptoeing around Joyce due to her unpredictability. The boys, sensing her mood shifts, grew cautious around her, especially when she displayed antisocial and negative emotions. Fortunately, such incidents were rare in the first year post-incident, allowing us a measure of comfort in our mostly harmonious coexistence. But in early 2022, everything changed once again.

The cost of living soared, hitting us hard just as we had begun to recover financially from our previous housing expenses and the pandemic. My business suffered yet another setback as people understandably tightened their budgets. My local client base dwindled, bringing with it a wave of uncertainty and anxiety, exacerbated by our living in a rental property. Joyce's intense separation anxiety meant she often accompanied us on trips when I visited clients. My husband would walk her while I worked, and a friend would take the boys out, ensuring all the dogs enjoyed some time apart. However, as my local work decreased, Joyce's time in the car with me lessened. We still walked the dogs together and separately, but the long drives with just Joyce ceased, and her behaviour began to shift noticeably. She became moodier, her emotions fluctuating daily, impacting the boy's ability to relax around her. They moved cautiously around the house, often seeking reassurance from us. Joyce began to control the spaces, growling at the boys for entering a room, looming over them on the sofa, and guarding random objects. Her behaviour outside worsened; she disengaged from our interactions, became brusquer with other dogs, and displayed confusing behaviours, initially inviting engagement only to swiftly rebuke them. Her demands escalated: she barked incessantly to go outside, then refused to re-enter, barked for constant snacks, and whined throughout the night, accompanied by relentless panting. Clearly, something was profoundly amiss.

Despite extensive veterinary checks, which yielded no medical concerns, Joyce's behaviour continued to deteriorate. Desperate for a solution, I consulted colleagues and medical professionals, to no avail. Our mutual attachment intensified, morphing into a co-dependent relationship marked by a form of separation anxiety on my part. I found myself increasingly homebound, anxious whenever Joyce was left with a friend or even my family. My focus shifted entirely to helping her, at the expense of my own freedom and finances. Joyce's interactions with Steve and Dave became increasingly concerning. She would barge into them, place her paw on them, or deliberately collide with them. Disguised as play, her actions were anything but playful. Indifferent to Steve and Dave's discomfort, she persisted until we intervened, redirecting her with a calm "Let's do something else; they're not comfortable with that." Her response was often to jump on the sofa, grab as many cushions as possible, and hump them, a clear sign of her inability to cope and her discontent. On walks alone, Joyce's demeanour would improve, indicating her appreciation for these solitary outings. However, her reactions to other dogs were unpredictable, ranging from amiable greetings to sudden, intense aggression. Returning from these walks left me emotionally drained, only to face Joyce's controlling behaviour at home, which kept us all on edge, frustrated, and fearful of potential conflicts. We were particularly concerned about the potential harm she could cause Steve or Dave.

Muzzle training was implemented as a precaution, but it was distressing to see Joyce shut down, and keeping her muzzled constantly at home didn't feel right. We found ourselves in a state of perpetual vigilance, always alert to the dog's locations and pre-emptively warning Joyce whenever Steve or Dave moved. Despite these efforts, Joyce struggled to adapt, unable to manage her reactions effectively. This period was marked by a palpable tension, the constant fear of a fight looming over us, coupled with the dread of the potential damage Joyce could inflict. Our household, once a space of harmony, had become a landscape of anxiety and uncertainty, leaving us grappling with the heart-wrenching reality of our situation.

It's a common misconception that such behaviour is merely a

display of dominance, but this is not the case.

Following extensive research and discussions with colleagues, we reached a consensus that Joyce was exhibiting a form of aggression that, while uncommon, was extremely serious: Control Complex Aggression. Although this type of aggression can be presented to either dog or people, Joyce had only ever displayed it towards other dogs, and never once acted aggressively towards people.

Joyce expressively showing how unhappy she felt.

Understanding the Issue

Control Complex Aggression in dogs is both challenging and serious. It manifests as seemingly unprovoked aggression, often occurring without clear behavioural triggers or warning signs. Dogs with this condition attempt to control their environment and interactions, displaying reactions that are extreme and disproportionate. This behaviour may stem from a dysfunction in the rage system of the emotional mind.

Characteristics of Control Complex Aggression

Dogs with this aggression typically show:

1. Low tolerance levels.
2. High irritability.
3. A tendency to anger quickly.
4. Elevated frustration levels.
5. Unpredictable behaviour.
6. A struggle to find contentment.

Behaviourally, these dogs might:

1. Stand over another dog or person.
2. Try to control the movement of others.
3. Physically push against another dog or person.
4. Guard random objects without a clear reason.
5. Subtly control others under the pretence of seeking affection.
6. Place paws on another dog's head, back, or shoulders.
7. Control access to areas like doorways.
8. Engage in intimidating staring at other dogs.

Identifying Triggers

Although this aggression can appear unprovoked, triggers often relate to the dog's internal sense of self rather than external stimuli. Common triggers include:

1. Handling or attempts to control the dog.
2. Efforts to stop or compel certain actions.

3. Removing or approaching a resource.
4. Disturbances, particularly when the dog is relaxed or around people or other dogs.
5. Being stared at.
6. Corrections and punishments.

Addressing Control Complex Aggression

Addressing this aggression centres around rebuilding trust and ensuring a safe, rewarding environment for the dog. Time is crucial; rushing the process can lead to setbacks.

Abandoning negative or aversive methods in favour of the CDD method and a non-confrontational approach is essential. Allowing the dog choice and autonomy in response to your methods can greatly reduce aggressive responses.

Given the unpredictable and extreme nature of Control Complex Aggression, it poses greater risks. A professional behavioural consultation is highly recommended before attempting any strategies, as typical solutions for other aggression types detailed in this guide may not suffice or be safe for addressing this more intricate issue.

Misunderstanding Control Complex Aggression as dominance aggression is a common error, as the issue is not about dominating.

The question that tormented me was: why did Joyce suddenly develop this problem? I agonised over what I might have missed or done wrong. Through deeper understanding, I realised this wasn't a sudden development; she had shown these tendencies since her early days with us. As a puppy in the cafe, Joyce displayed aggression when people entered, and though she eventually became indifferent to human visitors, her reactivity intensified towards other dogs.

Her overenthusiastic play as a teenager wasn't just typical adolescent behaviour; it was indicative of deeper issues. Joyce's background was unclear, but we knew she hadn't come from a reputable breeder or ideal home. Her arrival, fraught with issues, was revealing of her early life experiences. For years, Joyce had been signalling that something was wrong, but I couldn't accept that she wasn't content in our family. Now, at just over three years old and having passed through her major developmental stages without improvement, I had to confront a difficult truth.

Reflecting on the fight between Joyce and Steve, I realised something I hadn't been ready to acknowledge: Joyce had been happier as the sole dog in our home. Steve's return and Dave's later arrival must have been disappointing for her. The happiness I had observed in her when we first moved into our new home was not just because of a change in her environment but because she also believed she was living as the sole dog. Over time, her suppressed emotions and needs surfaced. When Joyce barked to go outside and refused to come in, it wasn't petulance; she was trying to escape from the boys. Despite their innocuous behaviour, she couldn't tolerate their presence. Her increasing depression, manifested in deep whining, sighing, and overeating, indicated her diminished joy, only briefly resurfacing when the boys weren't around. The boys, too, were affected; they became subdued, ceasing their playful antics out of fear of upsetting Joyce. Dave, once resilient and vibrant, was noticeably impacted.

Henry and I were forced to confront a heartbreaking reality: we faced three unhappy dogs. It became clear that keeping all three was untenable. Our small dog family needed to change. Leaving the house, we were overwhelmed with grief. The question loomed large: what could we possibly do?

We had already made the harrowing decision that keeping all the dogs together wasn't possible. Confronting this reality was gut-wrenching; I was overwhelmed with grief. The decision of who to rehome weighed heavily on us. It was an unfair choice; they were our family, and the dream was to stay together. Yet, what we wanted was secondary to what was ethical. Ultimately, we resolved that finding a new home for Joyce was the fairest option, a decision that felt like it would haunt me forever. If we continued as we were, the boys could end up seriously injured, or worse.

I was plagued with doubts. Would anyone else love Joyce as we did? Could they make the sacrifices we had made? What if she struggled alone? Would her new family understand her needs or would they leave her in distress? My head spun with worry; the thought of her feeling abandoned was unbearable. If it didn't work out, would she be passed from home to home, or worse, euthanised? My heart broke at these thoughts, and my husband was equally distressed, finding it difficult to even discuss it.

The process of rehoming was daunting. A rehoming centre seemed too risky for Joyce's specific needs. The thought of her in kennels was unbearable. I knew Joyce best and felt my profession and experience equipped me to find the right home for her. Not knowing her fate was unimaginable, so we decided to find her a new home ourselves, with the help of a knowledgeable friend.

We meticulously reviewed each enquiry, asking in-depth questions and being transparent about Joyce's issues. Despite her challenges, Joyce was a sweet, loving, funny, and sassy girl. One enquiry stood out: a couple who worked from home, had experience with dogs, and understood the challenges of a dog with a strong personality. We arranged a meeting, filled with doubts and uncertainties. My friend reassured me that we would know if they were the right fit upon meeting them.

When they arrived, Joyce's unusually enthusiastic greeting was a sign. She showed a comfort with them she rarely displayed. As they took her lead on a walk, Joyce pranced alongside them with a joy I hadn't seen in a long time. After two hours, I was certain this was the right decision. They promised a life of luxury and adventure for Joyce.

The transition was gradual, and a couple of weeks later, she left with her new family. The morning before, Henry and I took her for one last walk at her favourite place. I whispered my love to her, I kissed her soft golden head and told her I will *never* stop loving her, I struggled to hold back tears. Her departure left a profound silence in our lives. The boys didn't understand, and Henry and I grappled with our emotions. We tried to enjoy a day out and a quiet evening, but Joyce's absence was palpable. We missed even the chaos she brought.

Joyce's new family kept us updated, showing us how happy and free she was. She enjoyed holidays, swimming, and socialising with other dogs. Her behaviour improved significantly in her new environment. Seeing her thrive brought a bittersweet sense of relief; it was the hardest yet best decision for all our dogs. Joyce's happiness, albeit in a different way than we had hoped, was a testament to the love and care we had for her.

CHAPTER SEVENTEEN
- NEW CHAPTERS

In the days following Joyce's departure, the transformation in Steve and Dave was profound. Steve rediscovered his love for toys, romping around the house with a newfound freedom. Dave, too, found his voice again, embracing his playful and joyful nature. Both boys seemed revitalised, and their spark had returned. This shift was a revelation for both Henry and me; we hadn't fully grasped how much they had withdrawn in the previous months. Seeing them revert to their youthful, exuberant selves was heartening and provided much-needed solace as we navigated our emotional recovery.

Steve being goofy and playful again, shortly after Joyce left.

Dave's interactions increased significantly. He would bring us his bowl, placing it either on the floor or, at times, in my lap, as if to request a snack or a second helping. We had always affectionately referred to him as our 'little clown dog' due to his humorous antics, and it felt like we had our little clown back. Steve, on the other hand, showed remarkable progress with his reactivity towards other dogs. I worked with him, helping him understand he had choices: he could either avoid other dogs, observe them from a distance, or engage with them, depending on his mood. His responses varied, and sometimes he would become overwhelmed, especially upon seeing an off-lead dog. We would then calmly move away, shifting his focus. I learnt to accept his barking as a form of communication rather than a source of embarrassment. Most people understood; after all, Steve wasn't the first dog they'd encountered that barked.

In the weeks that followed, Steve gained enough confidence to greet well-matched dogs. We facilitated these encounters, always ensuring he was comfortable and the other dog was receptive. We would ask Steve questions like, "Do you want to say hello?" or "Are you ready to move on?" If I sensed he was becoming uneasy, I would gently encourage him to continue our walk. This level of socialisation, especially on the lead, was something we never thought possible before. Steve was learning to manage his interactions and began to exhibit less impulsive reactions. We even ventured to new places, avoiding areas with high dog traffic, acknowledging this limitation is a part of his personality. Although we accepted that Steve might always have certain limitations, the progress he made was beyond what we had envisioned with conventional training. Steve was discovering his sense of self, a development that brought us immense joy and hope.

Throughout our journey, with its myriad ups and downs, our appreciation for our dogs deepened, and our perspective on them shifted significantly. Reflecting on early videos from 2015, the contrast in how we interacted with them then compared to now is striking. I used to believe that with a force-free approach, I could train a dog to be anything I envisioned. This journey has taught me humility, patience, and a profound acceptance of who my dogs truly are.

Dave, whose interruptions when I spent too much time on the computer, once seemed like an inconvenience, now represent endearing moments. If he wants my attention away from my phone, I now embrace his hugs and kisses, putting aside the device. Of course, we've worked on his self-restraint for times when I can't immediately respond, and he understands when I say, "Wait a moment, let me just finish this, and I'll be with you." Steve's quick movements and intense energy, which used to stress me out, are now aspects I admire. I've learnt to embrace them for who they are, rather than wishing they were different.

By spring 2022, the escalating cost of living forced us into another difficult decision. Unable to afford our rental home and with my nascent business struggling financially, real choices had to be made. Henry returned to horticulture, leading us to move again, this time to the south coast. This change has been incredibly positive. The vastness of the beaches here has had a profound impact on our dogs. Steve's interactions with other dogs on the beach are the best he's ever had, and Dave delights in chasing waves and swimming in the sea, regardless of the season. They're happier and more content.

Dave loves to be involved with what we are doing so he is 'helping' us load the moving van.

Sometimes, the idea of the 'dream dog' – quiet, obedient, adaptable to any situation – is tempting. But this is just a fantasy. The reality is often different from what we imagine. We may think we know what we want, only to realise we already had it. There's no such thing as the perfect dog; it's a fantasy. While some dogs are quieter, more biddable, and more conforming by nature, being sweet, loving, and gentle, those who are less biddable, less conforming, and more rebellious often have important lessons to teach us. These dogs are comfortable enough to show us their true nature. Their cheekiness and individual traits are aspects to cherish. All dogs, irrespective of their nature, have something to teach us. They possess beautiful, wonderful qualities, and sometimes more challenging qualities are part of the package.

As we reflect on our journey with Steve and Dave, particularly after our move to the south coast, it becomes increasingly clear that having a dog is about so much more than basic commands or accolades. It's about the depth of the relationship we share, the give and take of daily life that forges a bond far beyond mere obedience.

Me with my two childhood dogs at the age of 15!

Me with my current dogs at the age of 26! Just at the beginning of my business in 2018.

Our experience has taught us that it's not just about their behaviour; it's about the strength of our bond. It's ensuring they feel secure and loved, affirming that they can be themselves in our presence. Do they feel safe and confident, not only in the calm but also amidst life's storms? Are we their haven, providing comfort and security when needed?

Being a dog parent extends beyond training. It's about nurturing their happiness, evident in the wag of a tail, the soft sigh of contentment. It's about our commitment to being there for them, reciprocating the unwavering support they offer us. This role encompasses meeting their needs in every aspect, from the nourishment we provide to the affection we show.

Throughout our time with Steve and Dave, the true reward has transcended the importance of perfect commands. It lies in the silent, understanding glances that communicate, "I'm here for you," and their gentle responses that reassure, "I know." This unspoken language, this bond we've cultivated, is the essence of what it means to have a dog. It's a beautiful journey, not measured by flawless obedience, but by the love and understanding that grow between us. This, in its purest form, is the heart of our story with our dogs – a testament to the profound connection that extends far beyond relying on training.

As I penned the pages of this book, I found myself uncertain about its title. I yearned for a name that encapsulated the essence and depth of our journey. Reflecting on the inception of my business, I fondly recalled the original name "Barking Up The Right Tree" - a suggestion from my mum that I cherished and used until the CDD method evolved into a tangible business model. This name carried not only a sense of identity but also a hint of playfulness and wisdom, qualities that have been a staple in my journey with dogs.

In choosing a title for this book, I wanted to honour that journey and the evolution it represented. Therefore, "Barking Up A New Tree" emerged as the fitting choice. It serves as a homage to my beginnings, a nod to the cherished advice from my mum, and a symbol of the new paths and methodologies that have shaped my understanding of and relationship with dogs. This title reflects the essence of our story - a tale of growth, learning, and new beginnings. It's a title that captures the spirit of moving forward while acknowledging the roots that have grounded and guided us throughout this adventure. "Barking Up A New Tree" is not just a title; it's a tribute to every step taken, every lesson learnt, and every bond strengthened on this incredible journey with our dogs.

CHAPTER EIGHTEEN – THE FUTURE OF THE CDD METHOD

As I've been developing the CDD method, my aspirations for it have grown exponentially. I envision this method reaching far and wide, impacting not just dog parents, but also professionals and enthusiasts in the field. My goal is for more trainers and behaviourists to embrace a naturalistic approach, one that aligns with the CDD method's principles, to help dogs thrive in a society often burdened with unrealistic expectations.

I dream of seeing more dogs overcoming their reactivity issues, more rescue dogs settling seamlessly into new homes, embraced with understanding and compassion. For puppies, I envisage a holistic upbringing that allows them to reach their full potential. To this end, I've developed several courses which I believe can significantly impact the way we assist dogs. These include a course for addressing reactivity in dogs using the CDD method, and a complimentary course aimed at aiding rescue dogs in acclimating to their new homes. Additionally, there's a comprehensive course designed for raising dogs, suitable for puppies, teenagers, and adults, all through the lens of the CDD method.

Looking ahead, my plans include creating a network of CDD practitioners. I aim to offer courses that enable other professionals to learn, adopt, and integrate CDD principles into their practices. This network will not only facilitate expansion and growth but also foster a community of like-minded individuals who can collaborate and drive change within the industry. The CDD method, with its adaptable and ethical training approach, is poised to redefine dog training and behaviour modification, transforming lives one dog at a time.

As I reflect on the journey with the CDD method, I find myself standing at the precipice of a beautiful vision, a future where our understanding and connection with dogs reach new heights of empathy and compassion. This method, born from a deep-rooted love and respect for these remarkable beings, isn't just a training technique; it's a movement towards a more profound kinship between humans and dogs.

Imagine a world where every dog is seen not just as a pet, but as a unique individual, with their own emotions, desires, and needs. A world where the bond between a dog and their human is built on the foundations of mutual respect and understanding. This is the future the CDD method aspires to create. It's a future where reactivity, anxiety, and misunderstanding are met not with frustration or despair, but with patience, empathy, and a deep-seated desire to understand.

In this envisioned future, rescue dogs are no longer viewed through the lens of their past traumas, but with hope and anticipation for the joyful lives they have ahead. Puppies are raised not just with love, but with a holistic approach that nurtures their entire being – their minds, bodies, and spirits. Adult dogs are given the chance to reshape and redefine their narratives, breaking free from the shackles of past misguidance or misconceptions.

The CDD method isn't just about altering behaviours; it's about transforming lives – both canine and human. It's about creating a community where every member, whether two-legged or four-legged, is valued and understood. A community where knowledge isn't hoarded, but shared generously, where success is measured not in ribbons or trophies, but in wagging tails, contented sighs, and the unspoken bond of trust and love.

In the heart of this community lies a network of CDD practitioners, a cadre of individuals united in their passion and commitment to this cause. These practitioners aren't just trainers or behaviourists; they are the vanguards of change, the bearers of a new era in dog-human relationships. They work not just to apply principles, but to imbue every interaction with the essence of the CDD method – empathy, understanding, and a deep respect for the canine soul.

As this method and its community flourish, we will witness a paradigm shift in how dogs are perceived and treated. We will see dogs living fuller, happier lives, and humans enriched by the unbreakable bonds they share with their dogs. This isn't just a fleeting dream; it's a tangible future, within our grasp, ready to be realised through the CDD method.

And so, as we turn the pages of this book to its conclusion, we also open a new chapter in the story of human-dog relationships. It's a chapter filled with hope, promise, and the unyielding belief that together, humans and dogs can create a world that is kinder, gentler, and infinitely more understanding. This is our vision, our mission, and our promise – for the love of dogs.

As we reach the conclusion of this journey, one that has been both deeply personal and universally resonant, it's poignant to reflect on the path we've traversed together. This book, much like the journey with our beloved dogs, has been a plethora of learning, growth, and profound realisations.

In these pages, we've journeyed through the nuances of dog behaviour, delved into the depths of their emotions, and celebrated the unique bond that forms between a dog and their human. We've navigated the challenges, embraced the joys, and discovered the transformative power of understanding and empathy. The essence of the CDD method, and indeed of this entire narrative, is about more than just training or behaviour modification; it's about building a relationship rooted in respect, love, and mutual understanding.

As I close this chapter, both literally and metaphorically, my heart is filled with gratitude for the lessons learnt, the moments shared, and the unconditional love experienced along the way. This book is not just a compilation of words and experiences; it's a tribute to every dog that has touched our lives, teaching us invaluable lessons in patience, resilience, and unconditional love.

The journey doesn't end here. It continues in every walk, every shared glance, and every quiet moment with our dogs. It lives on in the community of CDD practitioners and dog lovers who share this vision of a more empathetic and understanding world for our dogs.

To you, the reader, who has walked this path with me, I extend my heartfelt thanks. May the stories and lessons within these pages resonate with you, offering guidance, comfort, and inspiration. May your journey with your dogs be enriched with the understanding and insights gained from our shared experiences.

In closing, remember that each day with our dogs is a gift – an opportunity to grow, to love, and to understand a little more. Cherish these moments, embrace the journey, and continue to strive for a world where every dog is loved, understood, and valued for the unique individual they are. This is not just the conclusion of a book; it's an ongoing narrative of love, learning, and companionship – a narrative that each one of us is writing with our four-legged friends by our sides.

Thank you for being a part of this journey. Here's to barking up new trees and exploring new paths, together with our beloved dogs.

To find out more about the CDD Method, visit our website here: www.canine-dialogue-dynamics.com.

Raffy and I on a dream holiday in wales in 2013.

ACKNOWLEDGEMENT

As I reflect on the journey that has led to the creation of this book, I am deeply grateful to a host of remarkable individuals whose guidance, support, and wisdom have been instrumental in shaping my path.

Firstly, I extend my heartfelt thanks to the trainers and behaviourists who were pivotal at the start of my career in 2010. Your teachings, guidance, and the foundations you provided have been the bedrock of my growth and understanding in the field of canine behaviour. The lessons learned during those early years have stayed with me, continually inspiring and informing my approach.

To the mentors who have supported me throughout, your unwavering belief in my potential and your invaluable insights have been a source of strength and encouragement. Your willingness to share your knowledge and experience has not only enhanced my professional journey but has also deeply enriched my personal growth.

I am also immensely thankful to my peers and colleagues in the field. Your support, collaboration, and the shared passion for improving the lives of dogs and their humans have been a constant source of motivation. The sense of community and mutual learning that we have fostered together is something I cherish profoundly.

To the countless dogs and their humans who have crossed my path, you have been my greatest teachers. Each interaction, every challenge, and every triumph we shared has contributed significantly to my understanding and has been a constant reminder of why this work is so important.

Lastly, to my family and friends, your love, patience, and unwavering support have been my anchor. Your belief in my vision, even during moments of doubt, has been a source of immense strength. This book is not just a product of my efforts but a testament to the support and love you have all generously provided.

This journey, encapsulated in these pages, is a tribute to each one of you who has been a part of it. Thank you for your invaluable contributions, for the lessons taught, the wisdom shared, and the encouragement given. Your impact extends beyond the words in this book and resonates deeply in the lives of both the dogs and the people we strive to help.

ABOUT THE AUTHOR

Bethany Bell

Bethany Bell is a renowned dog trainer and behaviourist, celebrated for her innovative contributions to the field of canine care and training. As the founder of the Canine Dialogue Dynamics (CDD) method and owner of Canine Ethical Associates,  Bethany has established herself as a leading voice in the ethical treatment and training of dogs.

Bethany's journey in the world of canine behaviour began in 2010, marking the start of a decade-long quest to develop new, ethical ways to teach and understand dogs. Her approach has always been grounded in empathy and respect, focusing on the emotional and psychological well-being of dogs. This perspective led to the creation of the CDD method, a groundbreaking approach that emphasises communication and understanding over traditional command-based training.

Bethany's work is characterised by her deep commitment to ethical practices and her innovative approach to behaviour modification. She believes in nurturing a dialogue with dogs, understanding their individual needs, and fostering a relationship based on mutual trust and respect. Her methods are a departure from conventional training techniques, offering a fresh and compassionate perspective on how we interact with our canine companions.

Through her work with Canine Ethical Associates, Bethany has dedicated herself to promoting better standards of canine care and training. Her influence extends beyond individual dog training, impacting the wider field of canine behaviour and welfare. She is a sought-after expert and a respected authority in her field, known for her insightful, humane, and effective training methods.

Bethany Bell's passion for improving the lives of dogs and their humans is evident in every aspect of her work. She continues to inspire and educate dog owners and professionals alike, advocating for a more ethical, understanding, and compassionate approach to dog training.

Printed in Great Britain
by Amazon